# THE CRUCIBLE OF RACISM

# THE CRUCIBLE OF RACISM

## Ignatian Spirituality and the Power of Hope

Patrick Saint-Jean, SJ

Maryknoll, New York 10545

Founded in 1970, Orbis Books endeavors to publish works that enlighten the mind, nourish the spirit, and challenge the conscience. The publishing arm of the Maryknoll Fathers and Brothers, Orbis seeks to explore the global dimensions of the Christian faith and mission, to invite dialogue with diverse cultures and religious traditions, and to serve the cause of reconciliation and peace. The books published reflect the views of their authors and do not represent the official position of the Maryknoll Society. To learn more about Orbis Books, please visit our website at www.orbisbooks.com.

---



Published by Orbis Books, P.O. Box 302, Maryknoll, NY 10545-0302.



Manufactured in the United States of America

---

**Library of Congress Cataloging-in-Publication Data**

Names: Saint-Jean, Patrick, author.
Title: The crucible of racism : Ignatian spirituality and the power of hope / Patrick Saint-Jean, SJ.
Description: Maryknoll, NY : Orbis Books, [2022] | Includes bibliographical references and index. | Summary: "Ignatian spirituality as a formula of hope for today's antiracist struggle"— Provided by publisher.
Identifiers: LCCN 2021035133 (print) | LCCN 2021035134 (ebook) | ISBN 9781626984684 (print) | ISBN 9781608339303 (ebook)
Subjects: LCSH: Ignatius, of Loyola, Saint, 1491-1556. | Spirituality—Catholic Church. | Racism—Religious aspects—Catholic Church.
Classification: LCC BX2350.65 .S25 2022 (print) | LCC BX2350.65 (ebook) | DDC 248.4/82—dc23
LC record available at https://lccn.loc.gov/2021035133
LC ebook record available at https://lccn.loc.gov/2021035134

*I cannot send a copy of this book to my grandmother,*

*but I believe she is watching me now,*

*hearing everything and seeing everything from her place in heaven.*

*So I just want to say to my beloved "Tatie"*

*(as she always wanted me to call her),*

*this project is entirely dedicated to you.*

*You made me believe in life and gave me all that you had.*

*Because of you, I have become the man of hope*

*you always wanted me to be.*

*I love you, Tatie.*

## Contents

# Foreword

The first chapter of this book immediately captures the reader, as the author, Patrick Saint-Jean, SJ, connects himself with the ever-guiding spirit of his grandmother. He tells us that because of her, he became a man of hope. This book is a testament to that grandmother's prayer, that child's determination. As he develops his thesis, we see how that deep-rooted hope has sustained him across continents and ministries.

This is a powerfully prophetic book. I do not mean it is some ritualistic exercise in fortune-telling, but rather, using the restored original meaning of the word, it is "truth telling for the sake of the people." The prophet is possessed by a compulsion to utter warnings about the inevitable outcome of a people who seek a path of selfishness and individualistic priorities, who have a predilection to create enemies out of friends, and strangers out of those who would be family. But with those warnings comes always a vision of a blessed outcome when humility guides people to seek common bonds, to open themselves to discovering the rich gifts of those they encounter, and to become committed to the common good. In this book, Patrick Saint-Jean engages in all these aspects of prophecy.

He tells us that we must recognize that "we are all in the crucible" constructed by racism, and that that testing place is worldwide. He gives us the stories of those sent into his life, as true guardian angels, leading him on a path toward understanding, healing, and transcendence. In the most Ignatian way possible, he tells us narratives in which we can see the complexity of the social sins that burden us. And finally, he makes gentle suggestions on how to lose our fear and embrace our God-given gifts. The more we know, the more capable we are of saying "yes" to whatever call is sent to us.

Patrick's stories demonstrate that he speaks with the authority of his experience. Many of us—especially those who share membership in his religious community—will feel the pain he presents to us when he talks about the prejudices that have helped inform his training. What is to be remembered is this: the stories are only the prelude to the outcome. We hold in our hands the grace-filled result: the culmination of his grandmother's faith in him (as well as my own as his mentor).

And we read in these exhortations the firm faith that Patrick has in all those who will draw near to the fire of the Holy Spirit, sent to renew the souls of those who are called to be kingdom-builders with and for Christ.

— *Joseph A. Brown, SJ, PhD*

# Preface

I have often said that Ignatian spirituality and Black spirituality have much in common: a love for scripture; a relationship with a God who is not afraid to meet people "where they are at" and accompany them as they move forward; an invitation to see oneself as a partner with Christ; an encouragement to use imaginative prayer and contemplation; and above all, a very real sense that God is indeed involved in every single aspect of one's life—that "finding God in all things" is not just a fancy saying but a strong invitation to live our lives in a new way.

Being Haitian American, born in Port-Au-Prince and raised in St. Louis, Missouri, I needed something to ground my understanding of how to move in the United States as a Black person, an immigrant, and a woman of faith. Recently, I have felt a greater urgency. Yet, even in today's climate, Ignatian spirituality can speak to the question we voice or keep deep in our hearts: What do we do in the time of COVID-19, social unrest, and challenging political conversations when there are no clear answers? It is precisely into this arena that Patrick Saint-Jean steps forth to offer his story, his journey, and how the grace of Ignatian spirituality speaks into each situation and, most especially, into the conversation of racial healing and justice.

Patrick breaks his examination into three parts. First, he sets the context of what it means to be a person of color today. He wrestles with the fact that while there are definite privileges associated with his vocation and faith tradition, he can never escape the reality that his skin color determines the way he is accepted and allowed to move in this country. Even within his own Jesuit communities, he is confronted with the idea that being a Jesuit in formation is different from being a Black Jesuit in formation. Patrick could easily have let these unpleasant experiences turn him away from his vocation. Instead, he turns toward Ignatius and Ignatian spirituality to give him the language of not only how to respond to each situation but also how to "find God." He asks himself: What is the greater invitation at hand?

In the second part of the book, Patrick dives deeper into the ways in which Ignatian principles can help us all wrestle with issues of racial justice and healing. Simply identifying the struggles is not enough; more important, we need to find ways to enter into conversations and relationships with one another as we find healing and forgiveness together. Ignatian spirituality stresses the importance of being in relationship with God, with ourselves, and with others. Using the time-honored gifts of the Ignatian Examen, imaginative prayer, and *The Spiritual Exercises*, Patrick lovingly invites us to look at our personal experiences, find where we have invited the beauty of racial reconciliation into our lives, and where we have walked away from that invitation. But always, like Ignatius himself, Patrick reminds us that we are loved sinners, with the opportunity to "do better, because we know better."

In the third part of the book, Patrick models the gifts of *The Spiritual Exercises*, giving focus to the "weeks" as a way for us to heal from the woundedness of racism. Looking at the *Exercises* through the lens of racial justice and healing gives individuals the permission to be vulnerable and open before God, allowing forgiveness and discernment to guide how we move forward in love.

In these pages, you will find a personal outpouring and call to remind us of our possibility and promise. I am grateful for Patrick's honesty and his invitation to look squarely at the sin of racism—but not to be buried under its weight. Rather, with the help of Ignatian spirituality, Patrick invites us to answer the "call of the King" to follow Christ in this amazing work of racial justice.

— *Danielle Harrison, JD*
*Co-Director of Slavery, History, Memory and Reconciliation*

# ACKNOWLEDGMENTS

In a letter written on March 18, 1542, Saint Ignatius of Loyola stated that "the most abominable sin is ingratitude." Ignatius's words remind me that I need a deep awareness of the gifts God has given me through the people he put in my path on earth. This book is an expression of gratitude to everyone who let me get on their shoulders to reach a little higher than I ever could have alone, everyone who helped me extend my hands to work for justice, hope, healing, and reconciliation in the Vineyard.

History, spirituality, theology, psychology: This book is the result of strong communities from each of these fields, authors and researchers who stand behind me, who created the intellectual foundation from which this book grew. Thanks to each and every one of you.

Then, from its inception to its completion, this project would have never even begun without myriad wise friends, colleagues, family, companions, and acquaintances who faithfully devoted their love, prayers, and support to me during this process. Although my name happens to appear on the cover, I stood on the shoulders of several people while I formulated it, and I respectfully walked in their footsteps to create the book you hold in your hands now.

First, I extend a special, deep gratitude to my dear friend, editor, and colleague, Ellyn Sanna—Mother of Mercy (as I always call her)—who stood with me from the very beginning of this project and provided assistance at multiple levels. Without her, I would never have been able to finish this book.

I am also deeply thankful to Emily Sanna from *US Catholic Magazine,* who graciously introduced me to her mother at the start of this project. Emily, I will always have a special prayer of gratitude to you for sharing your mother with me.

A special word of thanks goes to my editors at Orbis Books. Thank you Paul McMahon, Robert Ellsberg, Maria Angelini, and everyone behind the scenes in this project, for the professional work that went into the production of this book. Your dedication, generosity, and passion for this project give me more hope for justice and reconciliation through an Ignatian lens.

I also thank those who gave me their exceptional support since the inception of this book. I cannot forget my dear friend, Henoch Debrew, who knew the genesis of this project and unceasingly encouraged me to bring it to light. I extend my gratitude to Lisa Kelly, who became my friend during this project, and my dear friend Jill Brown, PhD, who introduced me to her friend Becca, who also contributed to this project. Without them, this book would have never become a reality.

I have a special regard for Father Michael Christiana, SJ, my dear friend, mentor, and fellow mystic, who gives me a sense of home in the Society with his wisdom, mentorship, companionship, and friendship. Michael, your words inspired me at a crucial moment in this project to be a critical consumer of knowledge and a guardian of truth. In fact, I was only brave enough to write this book because of your encouragement and unconditional support while you were in a hospital bed. Your support and prayer helped me be the man of hope that Ignatius wants all of us to be. Thank you very much, King (as I often call you).

Words are not enough to thank my Jesuit community at Creighton University for their prayers and support during this project. While I am not able to thank all of them by name here, they were very generous to me with their patience and love. In a very special way, I thank Father Daniel Hendrickson, SJ, for his unconditional support, prayers, and companionship during this process, as well as my rector, Father Nicky Santos, SJ, for his support.

When I was asked to write this book, David Inczauskis, SJ, and Father James Martin, SJ, encouraged me to seek wisdom from the dean of my School of Arts and Sciences and the chair of Psychological Science at Creighton University. I followed their advice and requested a meeting with Dean Bridget Keegan, PhD, and the chair of my department, Mathew Huss, PhD. Both of them gave me their blessings, and they were consistently supportive of me during this process.

I am also eternally grateful to my students. Their hope gives me hope. They are my most important fans, always asking me how my writing is going. (Even on Saturdays, when I do not always want to see them, some of them pop in my door, just to say hi and ask about my writing.) I believe Creighton has the best group of students ever. Thank you very much, Bluejays.

In addition, I express my gratitude to the counseling department at Creighton. The director of the department, Jennifer Peter, PsyD, my dear friend Rebecca Thompson, PsyD, Bathia Supriya, MD, and everyone else were always there for me and very flexible about adapting my schedule during the writing process. The rest of the department were very generous with their care, support, and attention to me while going through this process.

I have been blessed with a community of dear friends, who never leave me despite my imperfections and failures: Maryelle Volanthen Campton, Charles Campton, Helen Evans, Esther Renterra, Georgina Gutierrez, Karen Cornejo, Martin Cornejo, Martin Alfonso, Jessica Mora and family, Josianne Joseph, Alice Olivier Préville, Duré Wilner, Nicolancia Bateau, Marlone Wilner, Darline Saint-Jean, Harry Saint-Jean, Celesson Saint-Jean, Dieu-Donne Sidor, Antonio Mondesire, Emma McCoville, the Gerrada family, and the Saint-Georges family. You are my long-standing fan club who have pledged to faithfully support me and walk with me no matter what happens on the road. A thousand thank-yous to my friend Melanie Garibay for her unconditional support to me in everything I do.

I could not have written this book without the backing I received from the Jesuits. We are a group of sinners yet loved by Christ and full of hope. The Society is where I come to meet a Christ who is actively working for love and justice. I am deeply grateful to Ignatius of Loyola who founded this company and to all my Jesuit brothers who contribute to this project on various levels. I thank my former provincial for his dedication to support Black Lives Matter, Father Brian Paulsen, SJ; my present provincial, Father Karl Keizer, SJ; my formation director, Father Charlie Rodriguez, SJ; my former novice master, Father Thomas Pip, SJ; my friend, Father Gregory Hyde, SJ; my former novice director and my friend, Brother Ralph Corderro, SJ; and my Jesuit companions, Conan Rainwater, SJ; Mark Blancke, SJ; Brother Mark Mackey, SJ; Christopher Alt, SJ; Josef Rodriguez, SJ; and Mathew Burk, SJ. All these individuals have contributed in one way or another to the realization of this project.

I have a moral, spiritual, and ancestral obligation to thank my community who have seen me grow, who are forming me for the mission: the Black Jesuits from the United States and Canada. Perhaps, today, I would have not been able to be here without them, especially Father Joseph Brown, my mentor, friend, and dear companion; Greg Chisholm, SJ; Father Renzo Rosales, SJ; Ricardo Perkins, SJ; Father J-Glenn Murray; Father James Pierce, SJ; Christopher Smith, SJ; George Quickly, SJ; Father Ike Udoh, SJ; Father Lester Love, SJ; and many more who have contributed to this work and to my life.

I think it might be considered a sin if I forgot my brothers from the Jesuit Antiracism Sodality (JARS) from the Midwest Province: Emmanuel Arenas, SJ; Father Thomas Bambrick, SJ; Aaron Bohr, SJ; Billy Critchley-Menor, SJ; Patrick Hyland, SJ;

Joshua Peters, SJ; and Damian Torres-Botello, SJ. These men form the backbone of this project, and without them, this book might never have been written. Thank you, my brothers.

It is very difficult, even almost impossible, to be Black and be in formation by yourself without a strong community that prays for you and with you and supports you no matter what. Today, I am humble enough to lean on all the shoulders of all these people whose names I've mentioned. I am grateful for the opportunity to continue to work with them for Christ's justice and love.

The last word of gratitude goes directly to my grandmother, to whom this text has been dedicated.

# Part I

# THE CRUCIBLE

## 1

# A Man of Hope

*To Christians, the future does have a name, and its name is Hope. Feeling hopeful does not mean to be optimistically naïve and ignore the tragedy humanity is facing. Hope is the virtue of a heart that doesn't lock itself into darkness, that doesn't dwell on the past, does not simply get by in the present, but is able to see a tomorrow.*

— Pope Francis[1]

Until I was eleven years old, I had never stepped inside a Catholic church. Then, when my Catholic godfather died, I attended his funeral mass. During it, I experienced a moment of epiphany that changed my life forever.

The words of the priest entered into me as though they were something physical. My heart began to race. The world looked suddenly different to me, as though I now understood new things, things that had never occurred to me before. I felt as though I had

---

[1] Pope Francis, "Why the Only Future Worth Building Includes Everyone," TED Talk, April 2017, https://www.ted.com.

stepped onto a pathway that I had never known existed. As James Baldwin said, "A journey is called that because you cannot know what you will discover on the journey, what you will do with what you find, or what you find will do to you."[2] That day—at my godfather's funeral—I set out on a journey that changed my life. I am still on that journey.

During the funeral homily, the priest looked out at us—directly at me, it seemed—and said that all of us had received a unique call from God. "God calls each one of us," he said, "to do something special in the kingdom of heaven." I didn't understand exactly what the priest was saying, and yet I knew his words were somehow meant for me. I felt it in my very body.

After the service, I asked my mother about the priest's words. She said, "The priest was talking about people who are going to be priests in the Catholic Church. You are not Catholic—so you don't need to worry about what he said."

I continued to think about the homily, though, and eventually, I talked to my grandmother, who was my best friend back then. She was a Southern Baptist minister, but she had also worked with a broad and varied religious community. She said, "My son, you are not Catholic, but I will pray for you, and God will provide." The hug she gave me filled me with a sense of peace and hope.

I was born in Haiti, where the second-largest denomination (after the Roman Catholic Church) is the Southern Baptist Church. My beautiful and loving family has been Southern Baptist for generations; my mother's family came to Haiti in 1875 to begin a medical mission and evangelize. Continuing her family's legacy, she was the main preacher in the church where I grew up.

As a kid, I often got into fights with my mother. I was curious about everything, and so I was constantly asking questions. Often she had no answer for me; instead, she would simply say, "Well,

---

[2] *I Am Not Your Negro*, Magnolia Pictures, 2017, https://www.youtube.com.

you will have to deal with your eagerness yourself. Go to your room and pray about it."

When it came to questions about social justice, however, she always made time for me. With care, love, and patience, she helped me understand the complexity of these subjects. Our devotion to social justice was woven into our family, and I understood that the community was an essential part of our identity as Christians. Both my parents are well versed in social ministry, and from them, I learned many things.

The person who had the strongest impact on my life, though, was my grandmother, Félicie Saint-Georges. She was my first role model, a model of love. Sharply intelligent, a nurse by profession, a Southern Baptist preacher by passion, and an avid politician and social worker, my grandmother taught me to be a man of hope. She believed that tomorrow will always be better; it is just a matter of waiting for what God will do. Equality, justice, and freedom were the themes of the songs she sang to me, and her love of community shaped my life. It inspired me to also become involved in social action and seek God in others through justice and love. I grew up believing that I was born to serve God in active ministry. But my family never dreamed where my vocation would take me.

For a couple of years, I did not speak further about the feelings I had experienced at my godfather's funeral. New ideas were waiting inside me, but I was busy with my life: school, church services, and the community. I had not forgotten, though, and the Divine Spirit was continuing to work in my life. I had a sense I was waiting for something to unfold.

My grandmother worked for the Haitian consulate in Paris, where she often met with various religious leaders, including Father Pedro Arrupe when he was the Superior General of the Jesuits. Father Arrupe's passion for working with Vietnamese refugees inspired her, and she had come to love the Ignatian way because of its commitment to social justice. She had also heard Father Arrupe allude to a Christ who was not a white man;

instead, said Father Arrupe, Christ looks like all of us, no matter our race, no matter our gender. Christ is each of us.

"Be open to God in everything," Father Arrupe said. His words encouraged my grandmother to persist in her work for justice. Ignatian spirituality does not discriminate—and through its lens, she came to see more deeply that standing up for those who are racially and economically on the margins is a spiritual practice.

"Learn to see Christ in everyone, in everything, everywhere," she taught me. Ignatian spirituality was helping her find a wider and deeper path to the Divine. Since I too was eager to learn more and follow the urging in my heart, she introduced me to her friend Father Moreau Joseph, a Jesuit who also taught in the school I attended.

I was thirteen, and he was eighty-two; I was Black and a Southern Baptist, while he was white and a Jesuit—but soon we were hanging out together as though we were simply two friends who could talk about anything and everything. Together, we created a place of hope, a place where I felt safe to explore the ideas I'd been pondering ever since my godfather's funeral.

Until his death in 2004, Father Moreau was my dear friend. Through him, I learned more about the Jesuit practice of finding God in everything, in everyone. Even on the path of suffering, he told me, I would encounter Christ. He showed me the way of justice, healing, and reconciliation that he had learned as a follower of the Ignatian way.

Perhaps most important, through Father Moreau's teaching, I came to see a Christ who is not white. When I found myself in all-white settings at school, he would say to me, "Stay on the path, Patrick. Hang on. Remember Jesus was not white." His words inspired hope in me, a hope I have needed more than ever in recent years.

Because of Father Moreau's influence, I was eventually confirmed as a Catholic. He helped me understand that the feeling I had carried within me ever since my godfather's funeral was

God's voice calling me to the priesthood. And all the while, my friend was teaching me more and more about the Society of Jesus.

### The Society of Jesus

Father Moreau told me that in the sixteenth century, Saint Ignatius of Loyola had helped found the Society of Jesus, what today we know as the Jesuits. Ignatius taught that we can encounter Christ in every aspect of life. He insisted that each of us needs to ask ourselves these questions:

*What have I done for Christ?*
*What am I doing for Christ?*
*What ought I to do for Christ?*

In the answers to these questions, the life of contemplation and that of active ministry are welded together. This practical, down-to-earth spirituality has remained at the heart of the Jesuits for nearly five centuries.

In his book *God's Soldiers*, the great English historian Jonathan Wright gives a good summary of the broad scope of Jesuit activity:

> They have been urban courtiers in Paris, Peking, and Prague, telling kings when to marry, when and how to go to war, serving as astronomers to Chinese emperors, or as chaplains to Japanese armies invading Korea. As might be expected, they have dispensed sacraments and homilies, and they have provided education to men as various as Voltaire, Castro, Hitchcock, and Joyce. But they have also been sheep farmers in Quinto, hacienda owners in Mexico, winegrowers in Australia, and plantation owners in the antebellum United States. The society would flourish in the worlds of letters, the arts,

> music, and science theorizing about dance, disease, and the laws of electricity and optics. Jesuits would grapple with the challenge of Copernicus, Descartes, and Newton, and thirty-five craters on the surface of the moon would be named for Jesuit scientists.[3]

This wide spectrum of professions and vocations all lead to the same destination: God.

### Ignatian Spirituality

Father Moreau taught me that Ignatian spirituality affirms that God is as close to us as the daily details of our lives. As the Jesuit poet Gerard Manley Hopkins put it, "The world is charged with the grandeur of God." We encounter God in the specifics of *this* moment, the *now* that is electrified by the Divine Presence. In other words, through active involvement in the world around us, we come to know God more deeply, and we also offer God our love in return. In the words of Ignatius: "All the things in this world are gifts of God, created for us, to be the means by which we can come to know him better, love him more surely, and serve him more faithfully."

Ignatius went even further. He taught his followers that as we become active in God's work, we participate in the presence of Christ in the world. In doing this, Ignatians focus on one goal: deepening their connection to God in order to become men and women for others. Spirituality—being in connection with God—is inextricably linked with service. And like my grandmother, Ignatius was a person of hope, a believer in possibility. He was certain God uses human beings to transform the world.

As my friend told me more about the Jesuits, I heard God's

---

[3] Jonathan Wright, *God's Soldiers: Adventure, Politics, Intrigue, and Power—A History of the Jesuits* (New York: Doubleday, 2005), 8–9.

call for my life even more deeply. Ignatian spirituality, I sensed, would be the bridge that I would cross to connect my heart with God. It would also become the vehicle through which I engaged with the world around me.

Jesuit formation is not a quick process. It requires about twelve years before we are ready for ordination. The length, depth, and breadth of this process takes stamina. But for me, the hard work has been well worth it.

Through the process of Jesuit formation, the lens of Ignatian spirituality has allowed me to focus more sharply on the work of justice. The teachings Ignatius left us do not create a philosophy or even a theology; instead they act as a doorway through which we can enter a new way of living in the world. Ignatian spirituality is a powerful tool in my work for racial justice, healing, and reconciliation.

Ignatian spirituality offers an alternative to the forms of Christianity that have been used to justify slavery and colonization, which, in their more modern forms, continue to be used to deny justice to the Black community. The white church has often cherry-picked its way through the Bible, ignoring scripture's clear and consistent support of those whom society has marginalized. Meanwhile, the actual message of the Hebrew Scriptures and the message of Christ in the Gospels and throughout the rest of the Christian scriptures challenge us to build a world based on justice, equality, and love. The teachings of Ignatius of Loyola give us practical ways to respond more deeply and effectively to Christ's call to an inner spiritual transformation that is expressed through social justice in the world.

This is not to say that this is the *only* spiritual tradition that supports the antiracist struggle. There are obviously many others, within both Catholic and Protestant Christianity as well as in other faith traditions, but this is *my* way. It is my doorway into the Divine Presence. It gives me the tools I need to do the work to which God has called me. Through the Society of Jesus, I lay claim to the identity my grandmother embodied: I am a person of possibility, a firm believer in the power of love. I am a man of hope.

For nearly five centuries, members of the Society of Jesus have been using the tools of Ignatian spirituality to lead people to Christ, promoting reconciliation and healing for the marginalized—but these same tools are freely available to everyone, not only Jesuits. Ignatius insisted that his teachings were not intended only for the clergy; they are also open to laypeople. Today, Ignatius continues to invite everyone—through their own experiences, whatever they may be—to *find Christ in everything*. Ignatian spirituality helps us know that God is at work, always knocking at the door of our lives. No matter where we are, God is there with us.

Included in the tools that Ignatius offers us are *The Spiritual Exercises*, a detailed structure for personal prayer and reflection, as well as the Daily Examen. We will spend more time with both of these in later chapters, but let me say now that the Examen lies at the very heart of this book.

The Examen is an open invitation to act with awareness, usually consisting of five steps:

1. Become aware of God's presence.
2. Review the day with gratitude.
3. Pay attention to your emotions.
4. Choose one feature of the day and pray about it.
5. Look toward tomorrow.

Each step is applied to life's practical realities, offering opportunities for contemplation, Divine encounter, and transformation. Ignatius encourages us to talk to Jesus as though he were a friend, opening our hearts to him. Secure in the knowledge that we are divinely loved, we gain the courage to be honest as we look into our own hearts. This is a spirituality that meets us where we are. It comes to us in quiet moments—and it stays with us throughout the busyness of each day. Whether we are at a protest, at the office, at church, on the bus, or in our beds at night, God is always with us.

As a part of the Examen, Ignatius encourages us to focus on the "interior movement" of our hearts, the "motions of the soul." These interior movements consist of thoughts, emotions, desires, feelings, repulsions, attractions, and imaginings. Ignatius taught that "discernment" requires a sensitivity to these movements, reflecting on them and understanding where they come from and where they are leading us. Through the daily practice of the Examen, we can discern our inner attitudes. We begin to see what is holding us back—and where God would have us go. At the end of each chapter in this book, I invite you to discern your own interaction with racism using an Examen.

### The Crucible of Racism

In my own life, the daily practice of the Examen has led me to a new perspective on my identity. When I joined the Jesuits, I also came to America, where I encountered something I had never experienced before: racism. I learned I am a Black man—and that America, including the Society of Jesus here in this country, is white space where people of color are often not welcome. This direct experience of racism became a crucible for me.

In the medieval practice of alchemy, a crucible was a container where different elements were heated to extreme temperatures in order to create an entirely new substance. For me, the racism I encountered after I joined the Jesuits generated a space of both fire and transformation, both deep pain and startling new hope. It began a process of transformation within me. As I write this book, I realize I am still dwelling within that crucible.

Recently, while talking with a friend, a fellow Jesuit, I commented that the stories that I use in this book to illustrate racism come mostly from my experiences with Jesuits in America. At the same time, I feel pressured to disguise the identities of the individuals involved in these incidents. My friend compared my difficulty to the sexual scandals within the Catholic Church. In the beginning, as the scandals came to light, the Church would not reveal the names of the men who had committed these acts of sexual violation. The underlying understanding was that by protecting the individuals, we were also protecting the Church. Then, after the Pennsylvania grand jury report, the Church was asked to release the names. As I listened to what my friend was saying, I recognized the accuracy of his comparison, and my stomach began to cramp. My head was spinning, my hands were sweating, and I felt as though I could not catch my breath. When I tried to speak, I choked. Tears sprang from eyes. My church, my own order, is still protecting itself rather than face the truth and bring renewed justice and healing into the world.

In writing this book, it is not my intention to complain about my fellow Jesuits. I know that they, like me, are imperfect human beings, struggling to live out their calling as followers of Christ, as well as followers of the path left for us by Ignatius of Loyola. I want to affirm all that is good about the Jesuits and testify to the good they do in the world. But at the same time I ask myself: *Why are we not allowed to speak the names of those who have mistreated Blacks? Why do we care more about shielding the wrongdoers than we do those who spend their lives on the margins of society? Are we going to side with the Gospel—or are we going to take our stand as "Christians" or as Jesuits, seeking to protect the "good name" of those identities? If we are truly followers of Christ, won't we follow his example and care more about those who have been abused and overlooked than we do the reputation of any group to which we belong? What would God have us do?* As I wept over these questions, I knew I was once more feeling the fiery pain of the crucible in which I live.

You do not need to be Black to live within this crucible. My experience is as a Black man and as a Jesuit, so this is the perspective from which I write this book, but you may have lived within some other branch of the BIPOC (Black, indigenous, and people of color) experience—or you may be a member of the LGBTQ+ community. You may have some form of physical challenge that has placed you at the margins of society, or you may be forced to confront ageism or sexism. Regardless of your race or gender, racism and the other "isms" that have shaped your life in some way, you too are in the crucible.

This book is for us all, because Ignatian spirituality can convert this place of fire—regardless of its form—into a place of regeneration. Through Ignatius's powerful tools of discernment, we can all—no matter what our individual experiences—come to understand more deeply what God asks of us from within this container of pain and possibility. Together, we can be transformed.

Despite the danger my skin color represents in the white spaces I move through, Ignatian spirituality has allowed me once again to live with the hope my grandmother taught me. Hope is fundamental to me; it is reinvented every day, and it underlies my thirst for justice.

As a Black Jesuit, I have learned to have hope in my brother Jesuits. I have learned to have hope for America and for our entire world. That hope, as well as my love for the Catholic Church, for the Society of Jesus, for America, and for our global community, is what has inspired this book. I write this book neither to protect nor to denigrate these institutions but because of my faith in their potential.

## The Structure of the Book

As you read this book, I hope you will join me on a spiritual pilgrimage of healing and hope. In the first part of the book, we'll discuss the nature of racism's crucible. In the second part, we will focus on how we can apply Ignatian teachings more specifically to the work of antiracism. Finally, we will go through the four phases of Ignatius's *Spiritual Exercises*. Although Ignatius divided the *Exercises* into weeks that can be practiced over thirty days, each "week" actually represents a stage in the process of entering into relationship with God through Christ. Each stage has a different theme, and we will apply each one to the crucible of racism.

In each of these chapters, I invite you to encounter a Christ who is yearning for justice, healing, and reconciliation. I pray that in all this you will hear God's call to you. Racism is a sin against the image of God in our fellow human beings, but antiracist work is a ministry of transformation. This is what my grandmother taught me, and this is also what I have learned from Ignatian spirituality.

We can't take action, though, unless we can breathe, for breath is essential to our life. In fact, it is so essential that we often take it for granted. The year 2020 taught us to look at breath differently, though. That seemingly endless year of pandemic, isolation, racial injustice, and protest made us aware of one another in new ways. We could no longer ignore the very essence of our lives. We discovered that we live in what I call the Age of Breath—a time when we are all being called on to learn once more how truly to breathe.

### Invitation to Discernment

Author Ibram X. Kendi wrote: "Hopefully, every individual will . . . look in the mirror, no matter the color of their skin and ask themselves the same question: Have I been challenging the system of racism or white supremacy or have I been upholding it?"[4] Through the following Examen,[5] we will begin the work

[4] "'Racism Is Death, Anti-Racism Is Life,' Says Author Ibram X. Kendi," interview with Eric Deggans and Audrey Nguyen, npr.org, October 24, 2020. Kendi is a leader in the work of antiracism and the author of *How to Be an Antiracist* (New York: Random House, 2019), and *Stamped from the Beginning: The Definitive History of Racist Ideas in America* (New York: Nation Books, 2016).

[5] Adapted from my "An Examen for Racism," June 22, 2020, https://www.jesuits.org.

of antiracism by taking a look into that mirror, examining how systemic racism influences our lives and how we engage in the sin of racism.

***An awareness of God's presence.*** Become aware of God's presence; sense his love and compassion. His love for creation is universal, encompassing the oppressed and marginalized. Notice God's presence, his love for creation, in the Black community and in other communities of color. Ask yourself:

- When have I failed to notice or respond to the needs of my brothers and sisters?
- Have I turned a blind eye to racial injustice? How? Why?
- How is my compliance, my inaction, and my sense of fear directly or indirectly contributing to maintain this structure?

***Review your participation in systems of racism.*** Now, review your day through the lens of racism. Recall your actions and thoughts with attention to how racism or privilege manifested itself. Often our actions are guided by our self-interests or personal biases, which can perpetuate harm. Sometimes, we see injustice and choose to detach from it, saying, "It's not my fight." Inaction is complicity, and it is wrong. For example, did you turn away from news about Black Lives Matter protests? Did you stay silent when a family member or friend said something ignorant or racist? Ask yourself:

- How have I been complicit in the suffering of my Black brothers and sisters?
- How have I benefited from social and systemic racism today?

Think about the community you live in, the social networks to which you belong. How have Black people been excluded from those spaces?

***Examine your emotions.*** As you review how you have participated in racism, pay attention to your feelings. Do you feel upset, angry, or uncomfortable? Confronting white privilege and racism is challenging. Sit with this discomfort. Feel deeply the plight of your sisters and brothers, and recognize your compliance in this suffering. Pray for guidance. Remember, we have the opportunity for transformation through the merciful compassion of God.

***Look forward.*** Antiracism requires active training and continuous learning about systemic racism. It is empowered by hope. Ask yourself:

- How can I leverage my privilege to uproot systemic racism?
- How can I use my privilege to make space for Black voices and other communities of color?
- How can I open my heart to make room for the transformation to the deeper love to which God calls us all?
- How can I become a person of hope?

Do not expect to have ready answers to these questions! Instead, continue to keep them in mind as you read this book. Allow them to be heated within the crucible of racism. Wait to see what new thing will emerge in your thoughts, heart, and life.

### Prayer against the Sin of Racism

*God, we recognize that racism is a social sin that has taken root in the garden of our hearts. We need you to convert us and purify our hearts, so that we can become agents of care, walking by faith in justice, hope, love, healing, and reconciliation for your greater glory. We know that racism harms your creation. Guard our hearts against it, and move us forward to enact change. Empower us to be people of hope. Amen.*

## 2

# The Age of Breath

*If a [person] lived, it was because God kept putting his breath, his "spirit" into this [person]. It was the presence of this Spirit of God that kept the [person] alive.*

— Anthony de Mello,
*Sadhana, A Way to God*

*Our grandfathers had to run, run, run. My generation's out of breath. We ain't running no more.*

— Stokely Carmichael[1]

On May 25, 2020, police officers arrested George Floyd, a forty-six-year-old Black man. A convenience store employee had called 911 to say that Mr. Floyd had made a purchase with a

[1] Stokely Carmichael, 1967 speech quoted in *Language Is a Place of Struggle* by Tram Nguyen (Boston, MA: Beacon Press, 2009), 40. Carmichael (1941–1998) was a prominent organizer in the Civil Rights Movement in the United States.

counterfeit bill. Minutes later, a white police officer had George Floyd pinned to the ground, his knee on Mr. Floyd's neck.

"I can't breathe, officer," Mr. Floyd gasped. "You're going to kill me, man."

Derek Chauvin, the officer kneeling on Mr. Floyd's neck, replied, "Then stop talking. Stop yelling. It takes a heck of a lot of oxygen to talk."

Mr. Floyd repeated that he could not breathe. He said it twenty-seven times. Finally, he lost consciousness. Officer Chauvin still did not remove his knee from Mr. Floyd's neck; he kept it there for more than nine minutes. By the time paramedics arrived, Mr. Floyd had no pulse. Paramedics did their best to revive him, but he was pronounced dead ninety minutes later.

Meanwhile, across the country and around the world, people were dying from the COVID-19 virus. All of us lived with uncertainty, aware that the virus could be deadly. While Black people had been on their knees for centuries, begging for breath due to the endless consequences of systemic racism, now they, just like many other individuals around the world, were caught in broken health-care systems unable to cope with a virus that robbed the breath from its victims' lungs.

Earlier in May 2020, shortly before George Floyd's death, one COVID-19 survivor reported: "It feels like you are drowning." A month after being released from the hospital, she was still on oxygen at home. "You are constantly struggling to breathe and to stay calm," she said. "When you can't breathe, it's all you think about."[2]

Another COVID-19 survivor described the same desperation to breathe. "I couldn't think or talk well because I was putting all of my energy toward breathing."[3]

---

[2] Anne Wallace Allen. "Covid-19 Survivor: 'When you can't breathe, it's all you think about," *VTDigger,* May 11, 2020, https://vtdigger.org.

[3] Michael Waters, "5 People on What It Feels Like to Have Covid-19," *Vox,* March 28, 2020, https://www.vox.com.

Without breath, we cannot speak.
Without breath, we cannot live.

### My Own Breathlessness

When Mr. Floyd was killed, I happened to be at the end of an eight-day retreat. The retreat had not gone well; I was going through a period of spiritual desolation that made praying difficult. I felt a deep distraction, a sense of dryness, a feeling that I was lacking the spiritual oxygen my soul required. When I told my spiritual director, he suggested that I take a break from the retreat and watch a little television. Like the good retreatant I sometimes am (though not always!), I turned on the TV—and discovered what was going on in the world. I listened to the story of Mr. Floyd's death in Minneapolis. I also heard about a white woman calling the police on a Black birdwatcher, Christian Cooper, in Central Park in New York City.

In the days that followed, I found it hard to breathe, and that sense of breathlessness continued throughout the summer. I prayed about my feelings, and I shared them with a fellow Jesuit. I explained that as a Black man, I was experiencing a deep fear after seeing what had happened on that same day in May to two Black men.

"That's nothing *you* need to worry about, Patrick," my Jesuit brother assured me. "Those two men were being problematic."

The implication was that George Floyd and Christian Cooper were to blame, not the white people involved. Rather than respond to my brother, I remained silent. I held my breath and returned to my room.

But I had many questions bouncing around inside my head. Was it possible that a white man's grasp of the situation was more accurate than mine? Did he have a better understanding of the injustice and suffering of the Black community than I did? Why did I feel as though the breath had been knocked out of my own lungs?

I knew that George Floyd was not the first Black man to cry out for breath; in 2014, Eric Garner had also repeated the words "I can't breathe" eleven times before he died face down on a sidewalk with multiple officers pinning him down. According to a report in the *New York Times*, over the past decade, the same phrase has been used more than thirty-five times by Blacks who died in police custody.[4] This knowledge was oppressive, suffocating.

I turned to Ignatius for insight into what I was experiencing—and there, I began to find some of the answers to my questions. Once more, the teachings of Ignatius became a doorway through which I could enter anew into God's work of justice and love.

### The Symbolism of Breath

In Ignatian spirituality, breath symbolizes both God's Spirit and the continuous gift of life. The breath embodies our ability to connect body and spirit. When breath departs from the body, so does the spirit. In that sense, breath is both universal and utterly unique to the individual.

Breath is not only essential to Ignatian spirituality; it is also a scriptural concept. The Book of Genesis tells us that humanity came to life through the power of the divine breath: "Then the LORD God formed man from the dust of the ground, and breathed into his nostrils the breath of life; and the man became a living being" (Gen 2:7). Job proclaimed, "The spirit of God has made me, and the breath of the Almighty gives me life" (Job 33:4), and the prophet Isaiah reaffirmed the message, saying, "[The LORD] gives breath to the people upon it and spirit to those who walk in [the earth]" (Isa 42:5). The Bible makes clear that breath comes from God.

---

[4] Mike Baker, Jennifer Valentino-DeVries, Manny Fernandez, and Michael LaForgia, "Three Words. 70 Cases. The Tragic History of 'I Can't Breathe,'" *New York Times*, June 29, 2020, https://www.nytimes.com.

Breathing testifies to the Divine Presence within each human. This means that when someone robs another human being of breath, they are denying that person's most essential dignity. Furthermore, they are usurping God's place. They are claiming a privilege that is not theirs to claim. To deny breath severs the living connections that are meant to unite us with God and one another.

Jesus experienced the denial of breath when he died on the cross (and he too was a person of color who was the victim of oppression and injustice). Death by crucifixion meant, among other things, asphyxiation, for the weight of the body pulling down on the arms made breathing so difficult that eventually the victim became exhausted and died. The Gospel account tells us that when Jesus died, he let go of his spirit—his inner divine animation—and breathed his last (see Luke 23:46).

The biblical words for "spirit" and "breath" are the same; *ruach* in Hebrew and *pneuma* in Greek. The Gospel of John tells us that the resurrected Jesus breathed on his followers and said, "Receive the Holy Spirit" (John 20:22); we could also translate his words as "receive the Holy Breath." With his breath, Jesus was empowering people who had been isolated and frightened, hiding from an oppressive government. With his breath, he commissioned them to go out into their world as a force for love and justice.

Every breath is a reminder of God's presence; every breath affirms the God-given value of each person's spirit. In other words, the struggle for breath is a sacred struggle. It is an expression of the Holy Breath seeking to find freedom in our world.

### The Challenge of Breathing

During the summer of 2020, as I turned more deeply to the faith tradition I love so much, I learned to breathe as a person who is seeking Christ. I realized that racism's ongoing refusal to acknowledge Black people as fellow human beings expressed not only disrespect for the Black community but also a disrespect for God and creation. By placing Black people into a category that is "other" from everything else in creation, racism denies the Holy Breath that flows through all. At the same time, I began to sense that, despite the ugliness of racism that has marred the Age of Breath, God continues to breathe through all things. I believe it was the Divine Breath that fanned the fires of racial protest, calling us around the world to speak out for justice.

Even as discrimination, fear, and injustice contaminated the very air we breathed, many of us were challenged in new ways. We began to pay attention to things we would have preferred not to face—the dehumanization of Black bodies and the lack of dignity granted to them. We could no longer turn away from what was now on full display. As Ibram Kendi has stated, "Literally, racism is death. And antiracism is life."[5] The Age of Breath has consequently forced whites to challenge their long-held belief that to be Black is to be dangerous and suspicious. This suspicion in the hearts of so many has led to murder, the physical denial of breath.

During my studies in theology, one of my Jesuit brothers helped me see the reality that Black people are too suspicious to be trusted. Widely popular in our order, this gentleman had been assigned to my community because of his wisdom and experience. He and I lived in the same house during his tenure.

Although this was a house of study, Jesuits at different stages of their calling lived there. My struggle to balance school and ministry meant I spent little time in the house. I taught two courses at a nearby university, helped in the parish next door, served as the chaplain for a soccer team, took four to six classes in my theology program, and tried to be a contributing member of my community.

---

[5] "'Racism Is Death, Anti-Racism Is Life,' Says Author Ibram Kendi," www.npr.org., October 24, 2020.

One night, I returned home at eleven, tired from a long day and longing for bed. My Jesuit brother was waiting for me, just as he had twice before in the same week.

"Patrick," he said, "where have you been? Why are you coming in so late?" Before I could explain, he went on to say, "I don't know if I can trust you. I don't think you're being transparent with me. Like so many Black people I've known, you seem very sneaky."

"Why do you think that?" I asked.

"Because you are never here. I don't know anything about where you go or what you do."

"Everything I do is what my mission has asked me to do," I retorted.

My Jesuit colleague could not see that God was breathing through me. To him, I was defined by the color of my skin—and that color made me inherently suspicious. When I finally settled into my bed that night, I could not sleep, even though I was exhausted. Instead, I lay awake for many hours, all the while feeling a tightness in my chest. Although my brother's words had not threatened my physical life, I still felt as though he had denied me my right to breathe.

Until the COVID-19 pandemic, breathing was something most white people took for granted. They may have never before realized the breathlessness that so many of us in the Black community experience daily. For centuries, people of color have had to constantly beg for oxygen, even though this is a gift that God grants freely to everyone. But now, in that breathless summer of 2020, whites were also called on to come face to face with the deeper significance of breathing.

### Breathing and the Black Community

Black people experience breath as a vital link with both the ancestors and the living community. The ability to breathe, in this sense, is something that no Black person can take for granted.

Too often, when we have tried to catch our breaths, we have been asked to defend and prove our right to our very existence, both as individuals and as a community. Denied this source of vitality and life-giving power, the community as a whole has been damaged, forced to limp more slowly along the path to greater purpose.

George Floyd's death was like an electric shock administered to the entire world, but at the same time, it was no surprise to those of us in the Black community. We have been forced to accept that the death of our own is a norm, something that has happened somewhere every day for centuries. As we walk through each day interacting with death, we are in a state of constant trauma. Somehow, though, we often become numb to what we are experiencing and prefer to turn away and think about other things.

The shock of Mr. Floyd's death forced us to open our eyes. We saw more clearly the reason for our own existence, and many of us knew we were being called to the sacred struggle for breath. Mr. Floyd's death revealed the state of breathlessness that we have been forced to inhabit for years. In response, the Black community took to the streets. We sucked in our breaths and not only spoke the truth; we shouted it. The heightened racial unrest continued for months.

We were no longer willing to wait to be heard. And yet several of my close Jesuit friends and colleagues—people I hold in high regard because of their intelligence and deep spirituality—have commented, "Patrick, why don't you wait before you write? Things will get better. Give the world time." The implication was that I should trust that time in and of itself would somehow manage to set the world right. As I struggled to respond to my friends, I found myself thinking of words spoken by James Baldwin:

> I was born here almost sixty years ago. I'm not going to live another sixty years. You always told me it takes time. It's taken my father's time, my mother's time, my uncle's time, my brothers' and my sisters' time, my

> nieces' and nephews' time. How much time do you want for your progress?[6]

When Martin Luther King, Jr. was accused of being in "too great of a hurry," he too experienced the same sense of frustration:

> For years now I have heard the word "wait." It rings in the ear of every Negro with a piercing familiarity. This "wait" has almost always meant "never." . . . But when you have seen vicious mobs lynch your mothers and fathers at will and drown your sisters and brothers at whim; when you have seen hate-filled policemen curse, kick, brutalize, and even kill your black brothers and sisters with impunity; when you see the vast majority of your twenty million Negro brothers smothering in an airtight cage of poverty in the midst of an affluent society; . . . when you are harried by day and haunted by night by the fact that you are a Negro, living constantly at tiptoe stance, never knowing what to expect next, and plagued with inner fears and outer resentments; when you are forever fighting a degenerating sense of "nobodyness"—then you will understand why we find it difficult to wait.[7]

King also said, "We must come to see that human progress never rolls in on wheels of inevitability. It comes through the tireless efforts and persistent work of men willing to be coworkers with God."[8]

---

[6] *James Baldwin: The Price of the Ticket* (Nobody Knows Productions, 1989).

[7] Martin Luther King, Jr., "Letter from Birmingham Jail," The Martin Luther King, Jr. Research and Education Institute, Stanford University, https://kinginstitute.stanford.edu, (accessed June 17, 2021).

[8] Martin Luther King Jr., "Remaining Awake Through a Great Revolution," commencement address at Oberlin College, June 1965, available at www2.oberlin.edu.

Ignatius of Loyola, who believed that we are called to complete the work of Christ in the world, would have heartily agreed.

Whatever the color of our skin, all of us have experienced the consequences of living in a world that has historically chosen to be unaware of some of its children. For centuries, people of color have been invisibly bleeding on the floor of systemic oppression, gasping for breath, dying from the thirst of repression, and starving from the lack of recognition and dignity. They have been the "least of these" of whom Jesus spoke (Matt 25:40), those who surprise us by revealing the presence of the suffering Christ in our midst. They challenge us all to be aware of their dignity. They demand that we face what we have become. And as Dr. King reminded us, they call us to be co-workers with God in the ongoing work of justice on the earth. This book is one way I am letting the Divine Breath act through me. It is how I have chosen to raise my voice for a justice that has been too long delayed.

## Breathing as a Shared Reality in Love

"To be just," said Father Pedro Arrupe, "it is not enough to refrain from injustice. One must go further and refuse to play its game, substituting love for self-interest as the driving force of society."[9] It is our lack of awareness of relationship of those around us—our neighbors, friends, brothers, and sisters—that perpetuates the system that underlies racism. Instead of sharing the Earth with people with whom we experience a bond of friendship and relation, we live on a planet that is limited to "me, myself, and I." Our own egos define the limits of our reality, and we seek to exercise total control over that narrow world.

The word *ego* is simply the Latin for "I." Freud, the father of psychoanalysis, defined it as that portion of human personality that we experience as "self." It is the part of us that interacts with

---

[9] Pedro Arrupe, *Men for Others: Education for Social Justice and Social Action Today* (Berkeley: University of California Press, 1974), 14.

the exterior world, the part that thinks and feels. Freud believed that each person also has aspects that the ego cannot normally perceive, and his student Carl Jung took this still further, affirming that while the ego lies at the center of our consciousness, the Self is a far larger construct, including what the mystics think of as the spiritual realm where we connect with the Divine.

Our egos serve a necessary function, but preoccupation with ourselves and our own lives can shut us off in our own tiny, individual realities. Cut off from those around us, we are also cut off from God. The ego can become a hard barrier that is impermeable to the Breath of God's Spirit. We lose the source of life and peace that our spirits require to live. We seek to control rather than embrace the Mystery of life.

Ignatius teaches us to abandon our egos to God, as if we were "lifeless bodies" that have surrendered their consciousness. At first glance, the twenty-first-century mind may find this directive unappealing, even unhealthy, but Ignatius understood what Jesus meant when he said, "Unless a grain of wheat falls into the earth and dies, it remains just a single grain; but if it dies, it bears much fruit" (John 12:24). By dying to our selfish preoccupation, we come alive in new and creative ways. Our breath becomes united with the Divine Spirit and with our sisters and brothers.

Ignatius expressed the meaning of this "death" with his prayer:

> Take, Lord, receive all my liberty, my memory, my understanding, my entire will—all that I have and possess. You, Lord, have given all to me. Now I give it back to you, O Lord. Dispose of it according to your will. Give me your love and your grace, for that is enough for me.[10]

---

[10] Ignatius of Loyola, "Suscipe," in *The Spiritual Exercises of St. Ignatius*, trans. Louis J. Puhl (Westminster, MD: Newman Press, 1951), 102.

In other words, we exchange our own limited concerns for the wider, more inclusive perspective of God. We learn the meaning of love.

As a Black man, I am not immune to the demands of the ego. I grow tired of being interrogated by police simply because my skin is black, and I am tempted to be passive and silent rather than speak up for justice. The fatigue of microaggressions makes me second-guess myself and doubt God's plan for my life. My quest for breath in the midst of protest, police brutality, pandemic, and political conflict sometimes drains me of life-giving energy. I beg God for breath, for life, for peace, but there are times when all I experience is silence. *Why is God allowing this to happen?* I ask myself. *Where is God in all that is happening?* I become so focused on the external world that I neglect my psychological and spiritual connections with God and others. My ego is in deep pain—but it is also demanding to be in control. Shut within its rigid confines, I gasp for breath.

As I lean into Ignatian practices, however, I discover new perspectives. These practices help me regain my sense of purpose, as well as my awareness of God's presence in my life. The practices become an anchor that continues to hold me steady and give me hope and courage. They allow me to breathe again.

Ignatian spirituality invites us to find the Divine Presence in everything, including our breathing. Each moment is an encounter with the God of life. Each breath is an opportunity for union with God.

Through our breath, we are also connected to each other. The Maori people of New Zealand express this reality in their traditional greeting, the *hongi*, which is performed by two people pressing their noses and foreheads together. In doing so, the breath of life is exchanged. Strangers are united. A spiritual reality is expressed with physical actions. It is a sign of mutual awareness through the breath.

As Westerners, however, we all too often fail to recognize this reality. Instead, we hopelessly search for connection in situations and possessions that can never satisfy our spiritual yearning. Often, we become disillusioned and cynical. Isolated within our own egos, we nevertheless grow to hate ourselves. We lose our sense of imagination and our trust in God's purpose, as well as our ability to love both others and ourselves. Our perspectives are narrow, and our breathing becomes shallow.

As this happens, we may try to soothe the discomfort with "transitional objects"—inanimate sources of comfort that take the place of the living Breath of God. The more we depend on these "soothers," the more we lose our ability to connect with the Divine within our own natures. Money, for example, can be used positively, as a tool to further our spirituality, but it can also dominate our lives, trapping us in a purely physical realm where God appears restrictive, distant, and even unreal. Other potentially good things in our lives can have the same effect, soothing our anxiety even as they condemn us to a fruitless search for peace and happiness.

The events of 2020 were shocking, ugly, horrifying. Rather than trying to soothe those feelings away, we are each called to open ourselves to new questions, allowing them to breathe through not only our minds and hearts but also our very lives. In answering these questions, we begin to see one another more clearly. We become aware of both the reality of others' experiences and also the challenge to be the people God calls us to be. Windows that have been stuck shut all our lives are now being thrown open, letting in fresh air. We are no longer silent, unable to speak the truth. We can begin to truly breathe again.

In my own life, the questions I faced throughout this process were painful and difficult. I asked myself: *What is the meaning of my life as a Black man? What does it mean to be Black and be alive in a world that perceives me as dangerous? How should we live creatively as Black people? How do we overcome the assumption that we present a danger to the rest of society?*

And perhaps the most urgent question in today's world: *How do we live as Black people in white spaces?*

### Invitation to Discernment

Ignatius does not ask us to turn away from the physical world; instead, he invites us to find God in everything. We meet God in smelling, touching, hearing, seeing, and tasting the world around us. The world only becomes dead, no longer breathing, when we seek to substitute it for the living Divine Presence, using some aspect of it to "soothe" life's anxieties.

This egocentric mindset is all around us and can be hard to resist. To break free from it, we can use a method of prayer taught by Ignatius, where we connect prayer with our breath. Praying with our breath is a form of incarnational spirituality, reminding us that our bodies as well as our minds can be part of our prayer. Since God created both body and soul, we can pray as much with the movement of our bodies as we do with the movements of our intellects or emotions.

*Become aware.* Take a moment to connect with your own breath. Be aware of the slow rise and fall of your lungs. Think of each inhalation as a vital connection with the Source of love. Surrender to each exhalation as an act of commitment to a life of love.

*Review your life and your emotions during the Age of Breath.* Now, as you continue to breathe in and out, allow your mind to connect with any experiences relating to your breath during the past couple of years. Ask yourself:

- When during this time did I focus only on my own selfish needs?
- When did I reach out to others?

Can you recognize the emotions you experienced in both cases? How did your actions of selfishness or generosity affect others' ability to breathe, both physically and spiritually? As you think about the "Age of Breath," can you identify ways in which your actions may have been caused by systemic racism? If so, how does this make you feel now—and how did it affect others' lives?

***Look forward.*** Once again, take a moment to be aware of the rise and fall of your lungs. With each inhalation, invite God to breathe Divine Love into your being. Surrender to each exhalation as a future commitment to a life of active love.

### Prayer

Pray for the grace to name my sins.

*Almighty and all-merciful God, give me the strength of spirit to name my sins and the courage to feel shame for them. Teach me to weep for the hurt and harm I have sinfully inflicted on others. Please, Lord, I really want to live aware of how I have let this terrible evil root itself in myself and in my world.*[11]

---

[11] Joseph Tetlow, SJ, *Hearts on Fire: Praying with Jesuits*, ed. Michael Harter, SJ (St. Louis, MO: Institute of Jesuit Sources, 1993), 23.

# 3

# Black Bodies in White Spaces

*Racism is not merely a simplistic hatred. It is, more often, broad sympathy toward some and broader skepticism toward others. Black America ever lives under that skeptical eye.*

— Ta-Nehisi Coates,
"Fear of a Black President"

*The process of healing also needs to include the pursuit of truth, not for the sake of opening old wounds, but rather as a necessary means of promoting justice, healing and unity.*

— Pope Francis,
speech given in Sri Lanka, January 13, 2015

During my early formation in the Society of Jesus, I undertook some special studies in theology that meant I had to drive to a different school. On a good day, it was a thirty-minute drive. Some of my classes ended at ten at night, which meant that by the time I packed up my books, chatted with friends, and left, it would be ten-thirty or almost eleven. Each time I left the building to go to my car, the woman at the desk would say to me, "Please, my son, be careful out there."

The South Side neighborhood I drove through has the largest Black population of the city. A white person might have assumed the woman was warning me about a dangerous neighborhood. That wasn't the case. Instead, she was cautioning me to be careful as I drove past the many police cars that patrolled the area. She knew that, as a Black man, I was in danger of being stopped, questioned, and possibly injured, even killed, simply because I was committing the crime of "driving while Black."

Every night, as I drove to my house on the North Side, leaving the South Side behind, the heavy police presence faded into nonexistence. The police obviously did not perceive that white neighborhoods required the same vigilance as Black neighborhoods.

## The "Danger" of Black Bodies

My experience demonstrates a painful reality: Black bodies are not only suspicious; they are also dangerous. They require the presence of police to protect whites. Areas where Black bodies are present must be constantly surveilled. Since the Black body is an ongoing danger, it must be watched, carefully contained, and separated from other bodies. This is why Black bodies are not welcome in white spaces.

Sociologist Elijah Anderson describes the phenomenon of white spaces as:

> Overwhelmingly white neighborhoods, schools, workplaces, restaurants, and other public spaces remain. Blacks perceive such settings as "the white space," which they often consider to be informally "off limits" for people like them. Meanwhile, despite the growth of an

> enormous Black middle class, many whites assume that the natural Black space is that destitute and fearsome locality so commonly featured in the public media, including popular books, music and videos, and the TV news—the iconic ghetto. White people typically avoid Black space, but Black people are required to navigate the white space as a condition of their existence.[1]

The segregation of Black bodies to protect white spaces is a long-standing historical fact. Its roots lie in the institution of slavery, when whites were well aware of the possibility of Black revolt. This reality required constant vigilance on the part of whites. In a letter to his father, written on July 24, 1841, plantation owner John W. Burruss asked, "Do we not dwell in constant danger, are we not standing, rather [lying] down—sleeping on a smothered—not extinguished—volcano?"[2] White people were unwilling to see that the volcano Burruss described was actually the flame of justice. Instead, they sought to maintain their "safety" by denying breath to the fires that raged constantly in the hearts of enslaved Blacks.

In 1836, Willian Drayton, an eminent United States representative from North Carolina, published an essay in which he made his case that Black bodies represent a very real peril to white spaces. Under the title "Unmasking the Evils and Dangers of Emancipation," he rejected the plea for justice, explaining that the "negro" will be much "happier" when he is kept out of "free space" (in other words, white spaces). He went on to say that the Black man "is happier, also, as a slave, than he could be as a freeman. This is the result of the peculiarities of his character."[3]

---

[1] Elijah Anderson, "The White Space," *Sociology of Race and Ethnicity*, January 1, 2015, https://doi.org/10.1177/2332649214561306.

[2] John W. Burruss to John C. Burruss, Reel 25, Micflm 105, ser H, Frame 00178, Burruss Family Papers, Alderman Library, University of Virginia.

[3] William Drayton, *The South Vindicated from the Treason and Fanaticism of the Northern Abolitionist* (Philadelphia: H. Manly, 1836).

Freedom and Black bodies, Drayton indicated, cannot exist at the same time in the same place. He justified his complacency with a hideous system by insisting that when Black bodies are prevented from entering free white spaces, they remain "without a complaint, or a cause of complaint," living "in tranquillity and comfort," while attaining "a degree of moral and religious excellence which in no other country or condition have they been able to reach."[4]

Men like Drayton lost their argument with Emancipation. But while slavery was outlawed, the perception that Black bodies were dangerous to white spaces did not go away. The perpetual stereotype is deeply rooted. As theologian Kelly Brown Douglas wrote:

> Free Black bodies have to be guilty of something. In fact, according to the web of discourse and knowledge spun by America's grand narrative of Anglo-Saxon exceptionalism, they are. They are guilty of trespassing into the white place. They are guilty of betraying their divine creation. Free Black bodies transgress both natural law and eternal law. Unless control is discussed . . . free Black bodies are bound to revert to their more "savage" nature and commit a crime.[5]

Black people cannot be trusted to freely go about their business without someone in authority checking on them. My Jesuit brother who felt the need to question me on my whereabouts is just one example of that; I was not trusted in white space, no matter how hard I worked to own that space. Unfortunately, "checking" often results in confrontation, which, as in the case of Mr. Floyd, can sometimes be fatal.

The world has far too often criminalized its Black bodies even as it has denied them the right to breathe. Paradoxically, a Black

---

[4] Drayton, *The South Vindicated.*

[5] Kelly Brown Douglas, *Stand Your Ground: Black Bodies and the Justice of God* (Maryknoll, NY: Orbis Books, 2015), 86.

person is not only seen as a body without presence, an inferior body that does not exist in the same way that a white person does—that cannot even breathe in the same way—but also as a body that is by definition a threat. Simply sitting in a car, as Mr. Floyd was, can be perceived as a danger to a police officer. Any movement of this Black body, even something as basic and necessary as breathing, must be screened and corrected.

### The Need for Freedom and Trust

For a body to be truly present, it needs free space and trust. These two elements remain in total contradiction with the existence of the Black body. Being Black requires that we engage in an ongoing battle for our right to exist. We are forced into a fight that demands that we be constantly alert, so that we can respond to anything that might trigger a white person's sense of danger. We cannot move freely. We cannot even breathe freely.

In the Age of Breath, the fires of justice were once more being fanned into life. The safety of those on the margins of our society is a concern that has risen to the forefront of our consciousness. Politicians spar over the needs of the Black community.

But will we in the Black community be trusted enough to make decisions for ourselves about our own safety? Will we be allowed to create our own accounts, rather than be confined by the old stories, the ones that were created through white insecurity? What are the Black stories that need to be told? What is the narrative of safety that must be rewritten about the Black community? When will we see that safety is essential to racial justice? Without it, we are still not truly free.

Freedom is a centerpiece of safety. Black people are not free because we are not safe. We are strong. We are beautiful. But we are not safe. We live in fear.

When I first came to the United States, I was "adopted" by a white family, whom I now consider to be my own dear kinfolk. My "mother" repeated the "talk" that every Black child receives at some point. She reminded me that as a Black man I was at risk. "If you get stopped by a police officer while you are driving, remember what to do," she told me. "Sit straight with your hands on the wheel. Do not look the officer in the eyes. Do not talk back to him. Wait. Do everything he asks you to do."

When I was studying theology in Chicago, this warning was always at the back of my mind. As Jesuits, we share everything in the community, so we do not own cars as individuals. Instead, we have a few cars that are available to everyone to sign out—something I needed to do each time I drove to class. I had been told that police are more likely to stop red cars than cars of other colors,[6] but often when I signed out a car for the day, the only one left was a red car.

I confided my problem to one of my fellow Jesuits. "It is very difficult to be a Black man driving a red car," I told him. "I do not feel safe."

"Are you sure you're not exaggerating the situation?" he responded.

I felt confused and conflicted. Once again, I realized how difficult it is for a Black person to be truly heard. From my colleague's place of privilege as a white man, he could not understand my very real fears.

I'm well aware that, even though I am Black man, I too am privileged in many ways. I have a strong network that supports me and, in some ways, protects me. And yet, whenever I am driving a car, I am always on high alert, constantly scanning for police. Each time I see a cop car, I remind myself of the advice my American mother gave me. This is the Black person's reality.

---

[6] This turns out be an urban legend that isn't quite accurate. According to the National Motorist Association, white cars actually get pulled over most often. Red cars are second. See Scott Huntington, "It's Not a Myth: Certain Colors and Makes Get Pulled Over More Often," *National Motorist Association* (blog), February 9, 2016, https://www.motorists.org.

### Black Experience vs. White Experience

The perception of safety—or its lack—is difficult to explain to someone who does not understand your experience. Not too long after the murder of George Floyd, I received an email from a white woman in which she commented, "I don't understand your concern about driving. If I feel unsafe when I'm driving, it's because I have done something wrong. If you obey the rules, you have nothing to worry about." I read in her words the implication that, if I feel unsafe in a car, it is because I am in some way at fault. Accusations like this, spoken or unspoken, serve to widen the gap between whites and Blacks, creating a dangerous chasm.

This Age of Breath in which we live has widened the crack, making it more obvious than ever. From the disparity of health services and educational opportunities to police brutality, the Black population is the greatest victim of this split between two realities. There is opportunity here in our new clarity, perhaps a chance to breathe in new ways, but at the same time, the white world's sense of its own identity has been threatened. The Black community is well aware of this, but because of that immense gap between whites and Blacks, their knowledge is not available to whites. Meanwhile, whites are unwilling to see their institutions as broken, severed by racism.

As psychologist Frantz Fanon[7] explained:

> Sometimes people hold a core belief that is very strong. When they are presented with evidence that works against that belief, the new evidence cannot be accepted. It would create a feeling that is extremely

---

[7] Frantz Fanon (1924–1961) was a psychiatrist and author from Martinique. A prominent thinker in the field of postcolonial studies, he was influential in developing the study of decolonization and the psychopathology of colonization. His work has inspired anticolonial liberation movements.

> uncomfortable, called cognitive dissonance. And because it is so important to protect the core belief, they will rationalize, ignore and even deny anything that doesn't fit in with the core belief.[8]

The Constitution of the United States requires the President to report to Congress on the State of the Union—and every year without fail, the President concludes the report with this conviction: "The state of our union is strong!" From the beginnings of America, however, when a quarter of its population was enslaved, that statement has always been, at best, a false narrative and, at worst, a bold-faced lie that denies the plight of African Americans.

In America, we would love to believe that the ideals and dreams of the United States, with its founding freedoms ordained by God, is a reflection of the fullness of the divine plan for humanity, the inalienable right to life, liberty, and the pursuit of happiness for people who are created equal. In reality, that promise has never come close to fulfillment. And we are loath to admit it.

To do so would mean accepting that we not only repeated the same crimes as our colonizer, England (and thus were no better than its monarchy), but that we ourselves continued to act against God's inalienable rights for all people. That is the failed promise America doesn't want to admit. Now, before our God, it is time that we do. The Age of Breath calls for it!

And yet America would still prefer to think of itself as a safe haven, a nation rich with business, education, and opportunity. Events during the Age of Breath reveal this to be a lie. Sadly, one result has been that many of America's citizens have become even more suspicious of each other. Different perspectives on what it means to be American divide the nation, just as they did in the years leading up to the Civil War. Meanwhile, too many of us are

---

[8] Frantz Fanon, *Black Skin, White Masks,* trans. Charles Lam Markmann (New York: Grove Press, 1967), 194.

unaware of our own obligation to take care of one another.

The Age of Breath will be an era that historians examine for many years to come. Recent events in America have had significance around the world, challenging other nations also to confront the reality of racism. Those who look at America from the outside are asking such questions as: *What was it that led America astray—and what keeps Americans separated? What makes them blind to the pain and circumstances of others? Why do they prefer to live in fear rather than get to know one another?*

### The Need for Open Communication

Unless we can find new ways to communicate with each other, I am skeptical that we will be able to answer those questions. We will have to surrender our attitude of self-preservation that depends on avoiding any conversation about race and racism. This defense mechanism serves only to perpetuate the misunderstandings that make it so difficult for Black bodies to venture into white spaces. It blocks the free flow of God's Holy Breath.

I have personally experienced this reluctance to talk openly about racism. My white "mother" is an immigrant from Belgium, and my white "father" is a native-born Texan. I have a room in their home, and they have always empowered me and treated me with dignity and respect. I would not trade them for anything in the world, because I truly consider them to be my family. However, despite that closeness, we avoid any subject that relates to race and racism in America. We pretend we are not dwelling within this very real crucible.

This attitude makes us live with a constant nervousness when we are together. We do not know how to expose ourselves. We each defend our own sense of personal security, even at the cost of hurting one another. Without any conscious intention of perpetuating the gap between Black and white, we nevertheless continue the narrative of division. As much as I love them, I am not telling them my true story.

The experience of being a body that exists but cannot be truly present in white spaces has been my story for so long. Feeling safe as a Black man is something I can only dream about.

I was not born with this understanding of myself, though. For most of my life, I was unaware of my Black skin. I had no need to hide it or protect it. That changed when I came to America and joined the Jesuits. It was then that I entered the crucible of racism.

**Invitation to Discernment**

Dr. Tema Okun, who has spent many years working for social justice, believes that antiracism is not a one-time decision but rather something that must be ongoing. She teaches six R's to narrow the chasm of racism.[9] I have adapted her teaching into the form of an Examen:

***Become more aware.*** *Read* and educate yourself on the effects, impacts, and other structures of racism.

***Review how you respond to your reading.*** *Reflect on* what this education means for you as someone developing an antiracist identity, such as identifying new ways to challenge everyday racism and work on racial justice initiatives. *Remember* how you participate in the thoughts, beliefs, and actions that uphold racism, whether you intend to or not, and how you "forget" that racism exists.

***Look forward.*** Take *risks* to challenge racism when you see it or realize when you are participating in it. Interrupt racial stereotypes when you hear them, and support people of color in your personal and professional settings when they speak out about their experiences with racism. Be aware that *rejection* is something you'll experience as an antiracist. Sometimes you will

[9] These six R's are adapted from Kenneth Jones and Tema Okun, *Dismantling Racism: A Workbook for Social Change Groups* (Portland, OR: Western States Center, 2003).

make mistakes and get it wrong when it comes to identifying and challenging racism. Learn to understand and accept rejection. Don't take it personally. Continue to stay in the fight against racism. *Relationship building* is an essential part of what you do along the way—with both white folks and people of color.

### Prayer for Discernment

*Grant me, O Lord, to see everything now with new eyes, to discern and test the spirits that help me read the signs of the times, to relish the things that are yours, and to communicate them to others. Give me the clarity of understanding that you gave Ignatius.*[10]

[10] Pedro Arrupe, SJ, *Hearts on Fire: Praying with Jesuits*, ed. Michael Harter, SJ (St. Louis, MO: Institute of Jesuit Sources, 1993), 55.

4

# A Microcosm of Racism

*In deep disappointment I have wept over the laxity of the church. But be assured that my tears have been tears of love. There can be no deep disappointment where there is not deep love. Yes, I love the church. How could I do otherwise? I am in the rather unique position of being the son, the grandson and great grandson of preachers. Yes, I see the church as the body of Christ. But, oh! How we have blemished and scarred that body through social neglect.*

— Martin Luther King, Jr.,
"Letter from a Birmingham Jail"

Before I joined the Society of Jesus, I was already a professional who knew the corporate world. I traveled in many countries, for both my studies and for fun. During these years, I experienced a combination of joys and struggles, but I never thought of myself as a "Black man," someone who was "other." I entered the Society full of experiences that had given me a sense of self-confidence. At first, I did not perceive myself as being different from the other men I encountered in the Society.

But among my Jesuit brothers, I soon realized I was a Black body in a white space. I began to understand that, in the United States, the Black body is always seen as a dangerous body and, therefore, an unfree body.

The first thing I noticed was that I felt as if I were invisible. At meetings, I was present at the table, but I wasn't truly seen. Those around me spoke freely, and their words were received with acceptance, even praise. I was reluctant to accept the old mantra that so many Black parents drill into their children's heads: "Be twice as good." (In other words, work twice as hard as your white counterparts—and even then, you may only get half as far.) I soon learned, though, that if I wanted to be heard, I had to follow the unspoken rules. First, I had to raise my hand for permission to speak. Second, I had to speak quickly and confidently. Third, I needed to be calm and cautious. As a Black man in a white space, I did not want to be perceived as an "angry Black man." Often, even though I raised my hand, no one noticed me.

### Being Black in the Society of Jesus

Black bodies that are invisible, like I was among the Jesuits, are unfree bodies. We Jesuits recognize freedom as a hallmark of Ignatian spirituality, and yet in the United States, a hidden, underlying assumption denies this right to Black men in the Society of Jesus. You may be permitted to enter this space if you are Black, but your experience will be different from that of a white person.

Please don't misunderstand me. I love the Jesuits with all my heart. My experience in the Society has in many ways been lifesaving, filled with grace as well as fun and laughter. But as I lived through the Age of Breath, I came to believe my life as a Jesuit was a microcosm of what all people of color experience when they encounter racism. This means that my own experience as a Jesuit is a tool for this discussion to which I have ready access. It serves as a lens through which we can focus on racism.

Despite its failures, I also love America. I have encountered desolation, isolation, discrimination, and microaggressions here—but also companionship, growth, and comfort. I am not ready to give up on America. As James Baldwin wrote, "I love America more than any other country in this world, and, exactly for this reason, I insist on the right to criticize her perpetually."[1]

The same is true of how I regard the Society of Jesus. Being a Jesuit has given me opportunities to work for justice—and yet we need to heal as a Society before we can spread this justice within our own communities. When we limit the freedom and trust we extend to our Black members, we fail to see the Body of Christ within their bodies.

While I was writing this book, a close friend argued with me about my premise that Ignatian spirituality is a powerful tool we can use in the struggle against racism. Black Lives Matter is a political movement, she insisted, and politics have no place in spirituality.

But the Society of Jesus has never seen spirituality as something that must be kept separate from the practicalities of life, including politics. Instead, the Society affirms that our engagement in politics can be a "powerful way we can work to uphold Christ's Gospel mandate to feed the hungry, give drink to the thirsty, welcome the stranger, clothe the naked and care for the ill and imprisoned with compassion."[2] The North American Jesuit Conference goes on to say, "As we respond to the call to be agents of change in society inspired by God's special love for those on the margins, we will inevitably be led into the public square to participate in the messy, urgent work of politics." This perspective is why I love the Jesuits so much!

---

[1] James Baldwin, *Notes of a Native Son* (Boston, MA: Beacon Press, 2012), 162.

[2] Jesuit Conference of Canada and the United States, "Contemplation and Political Action: An Ignatian Guide to Civic Engagement" (2020), https://www.jesuits.org/wp-content/uploads/2020/08/CivicEngagement-v10.pdf.

And yet, as a Jesuit, I constantly remember that I am a Black man. Often, those around me describe me positively: I am an *intelligent* Black man, a *well-dressed* Black man, an *exceptional* Black man. But before I came to America and entered the Society, I never needed these adjectives to define me and give me worth. My dignity was inherent to my identity, not something that set me apart from others who look like me.

When I first noticed this, I used to ask myself: *Why do people always talk about my qualities, what they perceive as extraordinary?* As time went by, I found the answer: this is just one aspect of how whites interact with people of color. It is how they overcome the dissonance they are forced to feel when they encounter a Black person who does not conform to their stereotypes.

"You know," one of my fellow Jesuits said to me at the dinner table, "Barack Obama is smart. A Harvard graduate. He's an unusual Black man." The implication was that Obama is not a *true* Black man. In my brother's opinion, Obama somehow manages almost to be a *white* Black man. His comment helped me make sense of what I had myself experienced.

But no matter how gifted and intelligent I might be, it was not enough to make me feel welcome. My skin was still black. I was still seen as "other." I was not considered to be human in the way that whites are human. As Frantz Fanon commented, "When people like me, they like me 'in spite of my color.' When they dislike me, they point out that it isn't because of my color. Either way, I am locked into the infernal circle."[3]

Before I joined the Jesuits, I did not know that the phrase "Black lives matter" had to be repeated again and again. Growing up, I took it for granted, a statement so obvious that there was no need to vocalize it. The crucible of my life as a Jesuit, existing as it does within the larger crucible of racism as a whole, has taught me that these three simple words need to be said over and over.

---

[3] Frantz Fanon, *Black Skin, White Masks*, trans. Richard Philcox (New York: Grove Press, 2008), 116.

This is obvious in so many ways, including the fact that Black people are twice as likely to be killed by a police officer while unarmed, compared to a white individual.[4] Black men are also 2.5 times more likely than white men to be killed by police.[5] But too many of my Jesuit brothers are blind to facts like these, just as so much of white America has been blind to the institutionalized racism that is alive and well within the United States.

I was not prepared for the crucible into which I was plunged when I came to America. I had been familiar with the Society of Jesus ever since I was a boy, and I had always loved it. The Jesuits I met while I was growing up were fun, smart, prayerful, and down to earth. I naïvely thought I already knew all I needed to know about Jesuit culture. Everything I had experienced taught me that the Society's focus is on hospitality and welcome, and I assumed this was a global characteristic. I never dreamed the message I would receive from many American Jesuits would be: "You are allowed to join us, but you are not welcome."

### The Jesuit History of Slavery

I might have been better prepared if I had reviewed the history of Jesuits' interactions with Black people. But as historian Dr. Shannen Dee Williams wrote, "The most dangerous weapon of white supremacy has always been its ability to erase the history of its violence and its victims."[6] This is true for the Jesuits as well. In order to face the reality of institutionalized racism within the Society of Jesus, we need to come to terms with our own history. Failing to do so allows racism to persist—unrecognized but all too real.

---

[4] F. Edwards, L. Hedwig, and M. Esposito, *Proceedings of the National Academy of Science USA* 116, 2019, 16793–16798.

[5] J. Nix, B. A. Campbell, E. H. Byers, and G. P. Alpert, "A Bird's Eye View of Civilians Killed by Police in 2015," *Criminology and Public Policy* 16, no. 1 (2017): 309–340.

[6] Shannen Dee Williams, "The Color of Christ's Brides," *American Catholic Studies* 127, no. 3 (2016): 14–21.

Here is the truth we can no longer brush under the carpet: The Society of Jesus participated in the institution of slavery in North America. Black men and women provided the unwilling labor that helped build and sustain Jesuit missions across the United States. Furthermore, Jesuit institutions profited from the slave trade.

In 1838, the university at Georgetown was in financial danger. To raise the money to keep it alive, the Jesuits who ran the university sold 272 women, men, and children (including a two-month-old baby) and sent them into the Deep South. Because the Jesuits saw God as white, they failed to acknowledge that these people were members of the Body of Christ. As Father Bryan Massingale has explained, the Georgetown Jesuits believed "that religion and holiness and faith belong to white people in a way it cannot belong to others."[7] The story of Georgetown University is just one of many within the history of the Jesuits' failure to see Black women and men as human beings who carried the image of God.

Like other white men of the time, the Jesuits rationalized the enslavement of human beings, insisting that slavery was the vehicle through which they were bringing Christ and salvation to Black people. They spread myths about their own kindness that still persist. In reality, however, historians have documented:

> Jesuits assaulted, manipulated, and overworked enslaved people just like any other slaveholders. People enslaved to the Jesuits regularly protested having their families sold apart; living in crowded, lice-ridden, poorly insulated housing; and having promises denied.[8]

---

[7] Bryan Massingale, speech given at the Association of Jesuit Colleges and Universities (AJCU) Commitment to Justice Conference, Seattle University, August 11, 2017, https://www.youtube.com/watch?v=Xq4Iz0SFMc0&t=2912s.

[8] Kelly L. Schmidt and Billy Critchley-Menor, SJ, "To Jesuits, Black

After President Lincoln's Emancipation Proclamation in 1863, Jesuit missions, like many Confederate states, refused to accept the decree. They continued to make use of enslaved people's labor.

Peter Hawkins was one of the many individuals who lived with this reality. Peter experienced the brutality of enslavement while living on Jesuit properties in Saint Louis, Missouri. He grew up seeing Jesuits flog the members of his community, possibly even his own parents. He was separated from friends and kinfolk when Jesuits sold them away as punishment.

Peter was a spiritual man, and in the Jesuits' eyes, he was "the best slave." He used their high opinion of him to persuade them to allow him to purchase his freedom. He continued to work for the Jesuits, however, in order to also purchase his wife Margaret's freedom. The amount he was asked to pay would be equivalent to about $20,300 today, a nearly impossible amount of money for a former enslaved person to earn, even though he worked night and day for two years. Finally, in May 1864, Peter requested a meeting with the Jesuits and begged them to have mercy on him and his wife.

The Jesuits discussed the matter. Later, they reported, "Peter . . . like almost all the other slaves these days, who have gone giddy, wants to leave us and live of his own right. But he had promised to repay us the money that we sent to buy his wife two years ago."[9] Reluctantly, the Jesuits came up with a compromise: They asked Peter to pay half of their asking price for his wife. They also gave him a choice about how he could earn the money. He and Margaret could either leave the Jesuits and live as free people, paying the money over time—or they could remain laboring for the Jesuits for another two years, after which, the Jesuits promised, he and Margaret would be able to leave as free people

---

Americans Were Objects of Ministry, Not Agents of Their Own Faith," *Daily Theology*, October 28, 2020, https://dailytheology.org.

[9] Kelly L. Schmidt, "Peter Hawkins and the Enslaved Community of St. Stanislaus," *Florissant Valley Quarterly* 38, no. 3 (2020): 1, 4, 5.

without further financial obligation. Peter and Margaret decided to stay.

Less than a year later, in January 1865, the Thirteenth Amendment was passed and Missouri state legislators also abolished slavery. At that point, the Missouri Society of Jesus made contracts with all their Black workers to continue working on the Jesuits' property for a salary. However, they did not apply this to Peter and Margaret, who continued to labor without pay. The Hawkins did not receive a salary until two years after the legal abolition of slavery. Peter's wages were fourteen dollars per month; Margaret's were five dollars per month.

This story makes my heart weary. I am both a Black man and a Jesuit, and so I must claim both sides of the story as my own. I, too, bear the historical guilt of failing to care for our people, for neglecting our vocation as followers of Ignatius of Loyola, and even more grievously, as followers of Christ.

And the Jesuits' racism did not end there. Although we never had a formal policy that denied membership to Black men, the practice of exclusion was common. This was the experience of Hermann Koch, who joined the community in Grand Coteau, Louisiana, in 1875, only to find that his Jesuit brothers refused to sit down and eat with him. The community soon sent him away. The reason for this action? Hermann was determined to have features "peculiar to the Negro race."[10]

Practices like these continued into the twentieth century, though they were hidden under new code words, including the concept of "usefulness." In 1944, Father Zacheus Maher, the American assistant to the Jesuit superior in Rome, determined that in regard to Black men,

> the basic principle in determining the admission of any candidate is not the good he may derive from

---

[10] Schmidt and Critchley-Menor, SJ, "To Jesuits, Black Americans Were Objects of Ministry."

> admission, but the good the Society may secure by admitting him. . . . Such a candidate ought not to be excluded merely because of his color. If, however, because of his color it is judged that he will not be useful in a given province, the effort be made to find a province in which he will be useful.[11]

The history of racism in the Society of Jesus could fill a book rather than a single chapter. Keep in mind, though, that none of these racist actions and attitudes were true to what Ignatius of Loyola taught. Ignatius himself practiced what he preached, refusing to yield to pressure from Rome to discriminate against Jews and Muslims. Policies changed after his death, however, and "pure blood" became a requirement to enter the Society, one that was not fully removed until 1946.[12]

### The Relevance of the Past

The argument might be made that all this happened in the past: Why should it matter today? When I tell my friends about Peter Hawkins, some of them say, "Okay, Patrick, I'm so sorry about what happened. But that was then, this is now. Don't get bogged down in the past. Let's focus on the future and work for a new reality."

Scripture contradicts this perspective when it says, "But take care and watch yourselves closely, so as neither to forget the things that your eyes have seen nor to let them slip from your mind all the days of your life; make them known to your children and your children's children" (Deut 4:9). This verse is written on the walls

---

[11] Stephen J. Ochs, *Desegregating the Altar: The Josephites and the Struggle for Black Priests, 1871–1960* (Baton Rouge: Louisiana State University Press, 1993), 395.

[12] John W. O'Malley, SJ, *The First Jesuits* (Cambridge, MA: Harvard University Press, 1995), 188–189.

inside the National Holocaust Museum, and it applies as well to the history of all racism. We have to look into the mirror of the past in order to confront what we see in the present. As James Baldwin said, "History is not the past. It is the present. We carry our history with us. We are our history."[13] If we want to engage honestly with antiracist work, we need the courage to look into the past. The past acts as a warning to the present. It matters.

What's more, the Jesuits' racist legacy continues to be felt. Today's reality still reflects the past. My experience of being allowed but not entirely welcome was one I share with other Black Jesuits down through the years. Clearly, the Society has struggled—and often failed—to live out its mission: to be the Body of Christ for *everyone*.

### A Black Jesuit in America

And yet I never experienced this before I came to America. As a teenager, I was so eager to join the Society of Jesus that I would have done so as soon as I graduated from high school at sixteen years old. This was not my time, though, for my grandmother, my anchor in life, was diagnosed with stage-four brain cancer. Instead, I began a twelve-year journey of professional preparation that led to me becoming a clinical psychoanalyst. All the while, though, I was thinking about becoming a Jesuit, and I kept close connections with the Society. I worked with a spiritual director and continued practicing my Catholic faith, while helping in each parish where I lived. Finally, I entered the Society, answering the call I had heard nearly twenty years earlier.

My heart had belonged to the Jesuits for a long time before I joined. During those years, I felt as though the Society were an old beloved friend, someone I knew intimately on a spiritual level

---

[13] James Baldwin, "Black English: A Dishonest Argument," as quoted in *I Am Not Your Negro*. Baldwin gave this speech at Wayne State University, an urban school located in Detroit, Michigan, in 1980.

despite never meeting in person. While I waited for the day when I could join the Jesuits, I didn't think much about race. Often, I was the only Black person in the places where I studied and worked, and yet it never occurred to me to define myself as a Black man. When at last I entered the novitiate of the Society of Jesus, I was a professional who was completely ready to close my business and follow Christ. I never guessed that this path would also lead me to discover the truth about the color of my skin.

The questions my fellow Jesuits asked me showed me they saw me as different, as *other*. "Can I touch your hair?" "How can you tell if you have a bruise?" "What do you people eat?" "Did you grow up with a bathroom in your house?" One Saturday, when I decided to make *legume de geroumon*, a typical Haitian soup that is very popular in my people's cuisine, one of my Jesuit brothers asked me, "Why is your food so smelly?" I realized these men found my food not only strange but also repugnant.

At the time, I had no words to describe what I was experiencing. I only knew that I felt oddly disconnected from myself. I began to question my place in the Jesuits. I asked myself, *Am I really welcome here?* Born into a loving and proud Black family, I had never before felt I needed to justify my Blackness. It had never occurred to me that I might not be seen and noticed in any room I entered.

### The Challenge of Black Identity

To be Black in America means to find yourself in a position where you have to justify yourself in order to exist. Ironically, through this painful undertaking, the Jesuits taught me to recognize and claim my Black identity. Today, I consider this to be the deepest spiritual experience I have ever had, full of grace and challenges.

As I recognized myself as a Black man, I became aware of the sin of indifference that acts as a cloak, hiding racism from view. I coined the term *jesuitica indifference* to refer to this state of mind as it thrives within the Society of Jesus. Indifference blinds us to reality. It disconnects us from others, obscures our understanding of their experiences, and smothers the living Breath of God in our midst. Indifference allows racism to thrive.

I began to see reality with a sharper clarity. The question that became clear to me was: As human beings, do we draw our identity from a patriotic sense of loyalty to a piece of land or a particular culture—or does our identity come from the presence of God in each of us? Ignatian spirituality called me to step away from merely reacting to the situation in which I found myself. With my eyes opened, I felt called to take action for change.

I stopped thinking about what I wished America and the Jesuits would be, and I began to ask myself, "What can *I* do?" I understood that the struggle against racism was embodied within Ignatian spirituality. I did not have to leave the Jesuits in order to be free from racism; instead, I could use the tools I found here to fight racism.

### The Presence of Christ

The presence of Blacks in America and within the Society of Jesus—and the presence of people of color throughout the world—is also the presence of Christ. Recognizing racial injustice in our midst allows us to recognize Jesus Christ among us. Christ comes to meet us in those who are broken, in those who are struggling for breath. Through our connections with other people, we connect more deeply with God.

And now we are invited to step past merely reacting to an unjust situation and begin taking positive action to build justice. For me personally, this means I am now fully engaged in becoming who Christ wants me to become: a Black man who is on a mission of healing and reconciliation. I do this with the greatest of love for both the Jesuits and America—but I have come to realize the truth of Frantz Fanon's comment: "Since the other failed to recognize me, there remained only one solution: to make myself known."[14] In proclaiming my reality, I also proclaim the presence of God.

The failure to recognize the Divine Presence in all human beings is an ancient one. It reaches back even farther than the day when the first ship carrying kidnapped Africans arrived in North America. During the civil rights era, however, Black people began to reinterpret their own identities; with that reinterpretation, came a sense of obligation to bring change—and that obligation eventually exploded out from the system that had maintained racism for so many years.

The year 2020 brought a new explosion. In a sense, the Age of Breath in which we live is a Calvary, a place of crucifixion, not only for me but for many others as well. It forces us to die to our indifference—and become aware of the reality that surrounds us.

### A Work in Process

With that awareness comes the unavoidable recognition that much work is still required. As the late activist Professor Vincent Hardin, in an interview on Krista Tippett's *On Being*, said:

> When it comes to creating a multiracial, multiethnic, multireligious, democratic society, we are still a developing nation. We've only been really thinking about this for about half a century. But my own deep, deep conviction is the knowledge, like all knowledge, is available to us if we seek it.[15]

As the Society of Jesus in the United States, we are also an undeveloped group of men when it comes to living and accepting

[14] Fanon, *Black Skin, White Masks*, 115.

[15] Vincent Harding, "Is America Possible?" Interview with Krista Tippett, *On Being*, February 24, 2011, https://onbeing.org.

people who are different from ourselves. As companions of Jesus, we need to be humble enough to see our need for racial healing. We need to pray for the grace to recognize that we all need to grow; we are all beginners, raw amateurs, when it comes to the practice of justice. We need to pray the Act of Contrition, which we repeat every day at Mass, with greater intentionality: "I confess to almighty God and to you my brothers and sisters that I have greatly sinned, for what I have done and for what I have failed to do. . . ."

But before we can truly repent, we must see and hear the experiences of Black people. Our lack of awareness has allowed racism to continue, both within the Jesuits and within the larger world. People of color continue to suffer, their existence denied, because of this lack of awareness.

In the fight against racism, awareness is the first step.

### Invitation to Discernment

The Jesuits are the crucible within which I have experienced racism—and within which I am still being shaped. From here, I am called to stop reacting and begin to act. Take a moment to consider how you can apply this to your own life through the process of the Examen.

*Become more aware.* Ask yourself:

- What is the crucible that I have personally experienced?
- What has shaped my ideas about race?

*Review your life.* Ask yourself:

- In what ways have I allowed indifference to hide the reality of racism around me?
- How have I reacted to racism rather than taking positive action?

***Identify your emotional response.*** Racism is a social sin, embedded within the structure of modern society, and we all bear its shame. Ask yourself:

- How does the call to repentance make me feel?
- Am I willing to hear this call? Why or why not?

*Look forward.* Ask yourself:

- What needs to change in my life so that I can better respond to racism in my world?
- What action am I willing to take to express my repentance for the social sin of racism? (Be as specific as you can, thinking of at least three concrete things you can do.)

**Prayer of Ministry**

*With new depth of feeling, I hope and pray, O God, that I can be more like Christ, the consoler, the healer, the liberator, the enricher, the strengthener. May I be able, through you, to help many; to console, liberate and give them courage; to bring them light not only for their spirit but also for their bodies; and bring, as well, other helps to the soul and body of each and every one of my neighbors. Amen.*[16]

---

[16] Adapted from the prayer of Pierre Favre, SJ (1506–1546), *Jesuit Institute*, http://jesuitinstitute.org.

# Part II

# IGNATIAN TEACHINGS

# 5

# A Doorway to Racial Healing

*Ignatian spirituality provides a framework for people of conscience who believe God has a plan for everyone to prosper. Ignatian spirituality also gives us a framework to understand racism is a sin that can exist only within structures of power, privilege, and oppression. . . . The good news is that we have inherited a spiritual tradition that has equipped us to disrupt whiteness.*

— "Ignatian Spirituality for All," *Alpha Sigma Nu*[1]

Ignatius of Loyola, who believed that we serve God best with a well-nourished body, insisted that his followers eat well. This is an aspect of the Society of Jesus I have always enjoyed. And so, one day while I was enjoying a typically excellent Jesuit meal, I was taken aback when I was once more confronted with the racism of a brother Jesuit.

---

[1] "Ignatian Spirituality for All," *Alpha Sigma Nu Magazine* 2 (2020): 7–8. (Alpha Sigma Nu is the honor society of Jesuit colleges and universities.)

"You are wasting your time here," this brother said to me. "Look around you—how many other Blacks do you see in this room? Face reality."

My brother spoke to me under the guise of concern for my well-being, which left me concerned and troubled. After dinner, I returned to my room, where I sat on the edge of my bed and thought about my brother's suggestion to "face reality."

I came to the conclusion that, number one, he was right: I am Black, and I wanted to be a Jesuit in a white province. Number two, he was right again: When I looked around the dining room, the only other Black faces I saw were among the kitchen staff.

As I reflected on all this, my thoughts turned to prayer. I found myself saying to God, "I am not going to leave—but I need a reason to stay. Just one reason." I remembered, then, that Ignatius of Loyola had overcome the odds when he created the Society of Jesus, and a term came into my mind, one that I had read somewhere: *possibility thinking.*

### The Possibilities within Problems

Leadership author John Maxwell has defined possibility thinking as "the willingness to see possibilities everywhere instead of limitations." He goes on to say that we need individuals who can see more than the problems we face as a society; "we need people who see the possibilities within the problems."[2]

"Possibility thinking" gave me the reason I needed to remain a Jesuit. I have seen this positive attitude grow throughout the Age of Breath, especially within the Black community. And, despite the faults within the Society of Jesus, I see this same energy at work there. I believe this is truly the leaven of the Holy Spirit, first planted in the Society by its founder, Ignatius of Loyola.

---

[2] John Maxwell, "Possibility Thinking," *John C. Maxwell* (blog), August 20, 2019, https://www.johnmaxwell.com/blog/possibility-thinking-part-one/.

**An Unlikely Saint**

Ignatius didn't start out as someone you'd think might go on to be a spiritual leader. Instead, he began his adult life as a courtier and soldier. He was, in fact, something of a lady's man, who let his hair grow to his shoulders in order to be more attractive to women. Historians report that he was passionate about fine wines and fancy clothes. His biographers describe him as a "man of vanities," full of pride, eager to be seen and admired.

All that changed when Ignatius was about thirty, after his leg was shattered by a cannon ball. His recuperation was long and painful, and even after two surgeries, he continued to walk with a limp. This was an enormous blow to the ego of a young man who had spent his life ruled by pride and vanity.

Forced to disengage from his active life, he turned to books to help him pass the time. He had always loved tales of chivalry and romance, but during his convalescence in his brother's home, none of these books were available to him. Instead, his sister-in-law gave him two very different books to read: *Life of Jesus* and *Lives of the Saints.*

As Ignatius read these books, his imagination was engaged. Instead of picturing himself as a heroic and handsome soldier, he began to wonder what it would be like to be a saint. Still full of zeal and enthusiasm, he turned his attention in another direction and decided he would work for God in the Holy Land.

God had other plans for him. Eventually, this vain man was so transformed that he became a priest. Now he focused his creative imagination and boundless energy on both God and others, rather than on himself and his reputation. As he gained spiritual insight and deepened his connection with God, he kept a journal where he made notes of the practices and prayers that seemed most effective to him.

Eventually, he gathered his notes together and created a carefully designed framework, called *The Spiritual Exercises*, which can be applied to anyone's life. The purpose of *The Spiritual Exer-*

*cises* is to facilitate the movement of God's grace within us "so that the light and love of God inflame all possible decisions and resolutions about life situations."[3] Ignatius organized the *Exercises* into four "weeks," but he did not intend that these would necessarily be actual seven-day weeks but rather stages on a journey to spiritual freedom and wholehearted commitment to the service of God. (We will be applying the four stages of *The Spiritual Exercises* to the work of antiracism in the final four chapters of this book.)

In 1534, thirteen years after his injury, Ignatius was ready to move into a new and deeper ministry. He went to Rome to ask the pope for permission to create a new order, the Society of Jesus. Six years later, Pope Paul III finally gave his approval, and the Jesuit order was born.

Ignatius used all his charisma and passion to lead the Society of Jesus, which grew quickly. During his lifetime, Jesuits were dispatched to India, Brazil, and Africa, and two Jesuit colleges were founded. The Jesuits also ran several charitable organizations, including one for former prostitutes. By the time Ignatius died in 1556, there were more than a thousand Jesuit priests.

That night in my room, as I thought about "possibility thinking" and the life of Ignatius of Loyola, I was struck by the way in which both circumstances and the Spirit of God had worked together to change Ignatius into a different person, a person whose ideas and teaching continue to shape our world today. I would have looked at Ignatius as a young man and dismissed him as someone too self-preoccupied to be of much use to God or others—but God looked at him and saw possibility.

I found myself wondering if this story of conversion, transformation, and reconciliation could also be applied to the work of antiracism. After all, I realized, God used the crucible of suffering in Ignatius's life to bring positive change to the world. Might not the crucible of racism have the same potential for

---

[3] David L. Fleming, SJ, *A Contemporary Reading of the Spiritual Exercises* (St. Louis, MO: Institute of Jesuit Sources, 1980), 5.

bringing to life something new, in my life and in the life of others, something that might lead to justice, healing, and hope?

The story of Ignatius of Loyola is more than a metaphor for the age-old struggle to surrender our pride and selfishness to become something better. As already noted, I have come to see a vital connection between antiracism and Ignatian spirituality. Because Ignatius was transformed, he gave us a legacy that is still practical and powerful today. His teachings are a doorway to antiracist work.

### A Spirituality Grounded in Real Life

The spirituality that Ignatius developed is not confined to the space within the four walls of a church. It is not limited to "religious" topics, but instead, it invites us to find God in everything. "He who knows God knows how to raise his mind immediately to God's love," Ignatius wrote, "not only when he beholds the starry heavens, but even on considering a blade of grass, or the smallest thing of any kind."[4] Every place and circumstance—from joy to suffering, from political protest to family life, from sex to friendship—is a moment of encounter with the Divine.

Ignatian spirituality is also a very practical spirituality. My friend and fellow Jesuit James Martin tells this joke:

> A Franciscan, a Dominican, and a Jesuit are celebrating Mass together when the lights suddenly go out in the church. The Franciscan praises the chance to live more simply. The Dominican gives a learned homily on how God brings light to the world. The Jesuit goes to the basement to fix the fuses.[5]

---

[4] Ignatius of Loyola, *Thoughts of St. Ignatius Loyola from the Scintillae Ignatianae,* trans. Alan G. McDougall, ed. Gabriel Hevenesi (New York: Fordham University Press, 2006), 43.

[5] James Martin, SJ, *The Jesuit Guide to Almost Everything: A Spirituality for Real Life* (New York: Harper Collins, 2010), 3–4.

Although this attitude can be carried too far—we Jesuits may become so focused on fixing the fuses that we forget that we are co-workers with God—still, it offers us a way to engage our spiritual beliefs with the real-life world in which we live. It inspires us to look for workable solutions. It teaches us that God cares about even the smallest problems, and that with Divine help, we can make a tangible difference in the world around us.

In the work of antiracism, this could mean working to provide public transportation to Black neighborhoods or getting grocery stores into what are known as *food deserts* (geographic areas where residents' access to affordable, healthy food options is restricted due to the absence of grocery stores[6]). It might mean working to ensure that your place of employment offers equal opportunities to people of color. It could mean having difficult conversations with people when you encounter racist comments. And it might mean taking to the streets in protest. What it does not mean is that we allow our actions to be controlled by fear.

### Freedom from Fear

In June 2020, a friend of mine invited me to attend a protest with her in downtown Chicago. I suggested that we should pray about it first, to discern how the Spirit of God might be leading us, but my friend responded, "No, I must go now because I am scared of what is going on in our country." I understand that feeling all too well, and I certainly do not condemn my friend for being afraid; as Black people, we always know that the next victim of racism might be ourselves. But the teachings of Ignatius warn against allowing fear to motivate our actions.

---

[6] For more information about food deserts, see the Food Empowerment Project, https://foodispower.org/access-health/food-deserts/.

Instead, Ignatius recommended that even as we become more aware of our emotional responses, we also detach from them. We do not allow them to rule our lives. Even while we live in a world that is dangerous, especially to people of color, we can experience freedom from the forces that seek to make us afraid. Ignatius wrote in the subtitle of his *Spiritual Exercises* that they are intended to be the means to "conquer oneself, and order one's life, without being influenced in one's decision by any inordinate affection."[7] What Ignatius meant when he referred to "inordinate affection" was an unhealthy attachment to anything, including our emotions, including fear. This is true freedom.

Often, we think about freedom as meaning we can do whatever we want, but Ignatius viewed freedom as being connected to what he called "indifference." By this, he did not mean the kind of indifference I mentioned earlier, an I-don't-care-and-I-can't-be-bothered attitude. Instead, he was talking about being detached enough from things, people, experiences, and emotions that we are free to set them aside if they don't help us "to praise, reverence, and serve God."[8] His concept of indifference is similar to what a Buddhist might call *detachment*, which allows us to be free from our selfish attachments to people, things, expectations, and ideas.

Ignatius's "indifference" is only possible when we interact with the world from a position of genuine love. He wrote:

> We should not fix our desires on health or sickness, wealth or poverty, success or failure, a long life or a short one . . . desiring and choosing only what is most conducive for us to the end for which we are created.[9]

---

[7] Ignatius of Loyola, *The Spiritual Exercises*, ed. W. H. Longridge (London, UK: A. R. Mowbray, 2009), 24.

[8] Ines G. Zupanov, ed., *The Oxford Handbook of the Jesuits* (London, UK: Oxford University Press, 2019), 76.

[9] Anna Abram, Michael Kirwan, and Peter Gallagher, eds., *Philoso-*

Ignatius taught that the end for which we were created is to love God and one another. If we practice Ignatian "indifference," we no longer focus on ourselves as the center of the world, and we let go of anything, including our own feelings, that doesn't help us to love God and others more deeply.

But fear gets in the way of love—and the Age of Breath has also been a time of great fear. Whites fear people of color; Blacks fear the police; people around the world worry about terrorism and crime;[10] conservatives fear liberals, and liberals fear conservatives; and everyone fears another pandemic. Fear is a normal human emotion, but it can make us unaware of one another's humanity. It makes us focus on ourselves and our own concerns rather than seeing the needs of our brothers and sisters. It doesn't leave space for God to act, but instead it can lead to violence and hatred. It stifles possibility thinking. Ignatian spirituality invites us to live free from fear.

This means that, if we protest, we do it out of love, rather than fear. If we speak out against racism, again, we do it out of love, not out of fear. We take action in love. We do not react in fear.

---

*phy, Theology, and the Jesuit Tradition: The Eye of Love* (New York: Bloomsbury, 2017), 19.

[10] A majority of Americans now worry that they or their families will be victims of terrorism, up from a third in 2014, according to a 2016 survey by the Public Religion Research Institute, while nearly two-thirds worry about being victims of violent crime (https://www.prri.org/research/prri-brookings-poll-immigration-economy-trade-terrorism-presidential-race/). A Gallup poll found that concern about crime and violence is at its highest level in fifteen years (https://news.gallup.com/poll/190475/americans-concern-crime-climbs-year-high.aspx). International studies have shown that around the world, about 50 percent of all people are "very worried" about terrorist attacks, and the majority of people are at least somewhat worried. See Angela Leite et al., "Who Is Concerned about Terrorism Attacks?" *Journal of Social Sciences* 8, no. 11 (2019): 316.

### An Authentic Faith

The Jesuits are known for being an intellectual and academic order—but Ignatian spirituality reaches past the mind, connecting with both the emotions and actions. In *The Spiritual Exercises*, Ignatius makes this clear when he asks us to pray about three categories of people. All three individuals have acquired significant wealth and now, concerned about God's expectations, they believe they should part with their money. The first person, however, postpones doing anything until the hour of her death; she is too focused on the concerns of this world to have time for spiritual matters. The second person rationalizes that God wants him to keep his wealth; intellectually, he believes that his money belongs to God but is unwilling to incarnate this value in his real-life world. Finally, the third person prays to be free from the attachment to wealth; this person allows God to use the money for the benefit of God's community on earth.

This exercise has direct application to white privilege and systemic racism. Like the first and second individuals, we may be unwilling to see that our attachment to our material comforts has a connection to racism—or that our participation in systemic racism has a spiritual component. We either postpone taking any kind of action against racism, or we rationalize away the call to take part in antiracist work. But as my Jesuit brother Ken Homan wrote, "Attachment to white privilege and white supremacy leads to an inauthentic faith. They are not open to the power of God's justice."[11] Ignatius calls us to work actively in collaboration with God for justice.

As a Jesuit, I live and breathe Ignatian spirituality. It has become the doorway through which I see possibility in a world that is broken by racism. It empowers me to trust in a better future. Despite its human flaws, the Society of Jesus is a vehicle of

---

[11] Ken Homan, SJ, "What Dr. King and St. Ignatius Taught Me about Discernment and Anti-Racism," *Jesuit Post,* January 18, 2021, https://thejesuitpost.org.

justice. It maintains its roots in the teachings of Ignatius, affirming that we are all *friends in the Lord.* Living in the Jesuit community, I have experienced firsthand honest, healthy friendships with people who share my commitment to work for justice.

But I am not writing this book only for other Jesuits to read. As Ignatius himself taught, this is a spirituality that is available to everyone; you do not have to join the Society of Jesus to practice Ignatius's practical approach that integrates emotions with intellect, contemplation with action, and love of God with love for other human beings.

No one can claim to be immune to racism; its patterns are indelibly imprinted on our thoughts and actions. But Ignatius insisted that we are "lovable sinners" who can be changed by the love and grace of God. Ignatian spirituality is about possibility thinking. It refuses to be confined by societal expectations; it looks past appearances. It perceives a deeper reality—and that reality becomes a call to action. This requires a conscious choice on our part.

*Be alert*, Ignatius taught. *Be aware*. Pay attention to wherever you find the Presence of God. See the Divine Presence in those who are different from you and in those who are suffering from poverty and societal injustice. Don't overlook any brother or sister, because everyone—no matter how dissimilar to you they may seem—carries the image of God. To ignore the experience of any part of the human family is to ignore an aspect of God.

Awareness is the process by which we open ourselves to Divine Love. This intentional awareness is the hallmark of Ignatian spirituality. Through awareness, we step out of our selfish fears and into the security of God's love. In doing so, we lose our self-absorption and become more aware of the needs of others.

Awareness is the foundation of antiracism. It empowers us to see the possibilities that lead to justice.

### Invitation to Discernment

Harriet Tubman, the great abolitionist, is often quoted as saying, "Every great dream begins with a dreamer. Always remember, you have within you the strength, the patience, and the passion to reach for the stars to change the world."[12] Ignatian spirituality believes that God speaks to us through our deepest desires, the dreams that inspire us to work for a better future. Use this Examen as an opportunity to focus on your dreams.

*Become aware.* Take a quiet moment to become aware of the dreams that motivate your life. Now ask yourself:

- Are my dreams fueled by my ego—or by compassion?

*Review your life with gratitude.* Ask yourself:

- What dreams has God already fulfilled in my life?
- What new dreams might God be calling me toward?

*Look forward.* Working to make a dream come true is always a risk. I dream of a more just world for people of color—and I am taking a risk by opening myself to you through this book, inviting you to join me in the spirit of togetherness. Ask yourself:

- Am I willing to let go of my self-interest in order to experience the suffering of others?
- What risks am I willing to take on their behalf?
- Can I dare to dream a bigger dream, one that encompasses the needs of others?

---

[12] It turns out that there is no historical evidence that Harriet Tubman actually spoke or wrote these sentences. However, we do know that dreams were important in her life, and they helped to inspire her to take action on behalf of her people.

**Prayer**

*Lord, Jesus Christ, who reached across the ethnic boundaries between Samaritan, Roman, and Jew, who offered fresh sight to the blind and freedom to captives, help us break down the barriers in our community, enable us to see the reality of racism and bigotry, and free us to challenge and uproot it from ourselves, our society and our world. Amen.*[13]

[13] John Bucki, SJ, *Social Justice Resource Center*, https://socialjusticeresourcecenter.org/prayers/racism/.

# 6

# Awareness

*Real change will come when it is brought about, not by your ego, but by reality. Awareness releases reality to change you.*

— Anthony de Mello, *Awareness*

*Awareness should be the status quo. It should be the baseline expectation for those of us who claim to be committed to social justice. . . . The information is out there, the voices are loud, and it is everyone's responsibility to listen.*

— Adam Foley, "Social Justice: Moving from Awareness to Action"

"I don't see color." This was what a close friend of mine said to me not long ago. "Therefore," he continued, "I am not a racist."

I tried to counter his words to explain why his position was not a viable option in the conversation about race, but eventually, he turned his back and walked away from me. His response was so blunt, so cold, that I spent the rest of that day feeling confused and sad. Once again, racism had robbed the breath from my lungs. Once again, I felt as though I were invisible.

I found myself thinking of these lines from James Baldwin:

> American white men still nourish the illusion that there is some means of recovering the European innocence, of returning to a state in which Black men do not exist. This is one of the greatest errors Americans can make. The identity they fought so hard to protect has, by virtue of that battle, undergone a change: Americans are as unlike any other white people in the world as it is possible to be. . . . This vision of the world is dangerously inaccurate, and perfectly useless. For it protects our moral high-mindedness at the terrible expense of weakening our grasp of reality. People who shut their eyes to reality simply invite their own destruction, and anyone who insists on remaining in a state of innocence long after that innocence is dead turns himself into a monster.[1]

### Opening Our Eyes to Reality

When white people insist they don't "see color," they are hiding behind their refusal to see reality. They are claiming an innocence that does not exist. Today, awareness is indispensable for any antiracist work. We must begin to see. As followers of Christ, we have a moral obligation to embrace this invitation as a spiritual way of responding to our vocation as God's creatures.

Do you truly see Black people? Are you aware of their reality? These questions are at the heart of racial justice.

Even as a Black man, I had to answer these same questions. When I was in my early formation as a Jesuit, I too was guilty

---

[1] James Baldwin, *The Price of the Ticket: Collected Nonfiction, 1948–1985* (New York: St. Martin's Press, 1985), 89.

of closing my eyes to reality. You might say that I was both the victim and the oppressor at the same time. I did not stand up for my people, and I allowed myself to be comfortable with the institutionalized racism that surrounded me.

In 2016, police killed Philando Castile, a thirty-two-year-old Black man, at a routine traffic stop just a couple of miles from where I was living in Minneapolis at the time. In the days afterward, protesters gathered at the nearby Governor's House, but I did not join them. I also lived exactly half a mile from St. Peter Claver Parish, a Black, socially active congregation, but I never went there to contribute to their ministry. Instead, I numbed myself, becoming a hyperactive workaholic, all my energy committed to other ministries.

I was always busy, doing everything I could—and at the same time, I was constantly doing less than what I most needed to do: raise my awareness of my people, the Black community. Somehow, I went to bed each night, easily, with no regret. Lost in the illusion of self-sufficiency, I was not yet open to being pierced by the sin of racism. I was unwilling to face even the reality of my own loneliness and sense of rejection.

I was experiencing a dual reality. On the one hand, I was well aware of the microaggressions and discrimination I personally faced. On the other hand, I allowed myself to become numb to the pain.

Eventually, I suffered a long period of desolation. While I had felt and responded to a call from Christ to join the Society of Jesus, in that early period, I constantly felt a sense of lack. I had joined the Jesuits blindly, unaware of their racism. Now, I was paying for that ignorance. And yet I allowed it to continue by becoming numb to the humiliations I suffered (such as the time when a fellow Jesuit predicted I would be miserable in the Society because Blacks lack the stamina to pursue their Jesuit formation). I joined in singing "All Are Welcome" at Mass every day, unwilling to recognize that the first and most important element of genuine welcome is seeing Christ's image in each other. I reacted to this situation by allowing a part of myself to become dead. Denying myself the energy of Divine Breath, I was unable to step forward and act.

Reaction is done out of fear, not freedom, and not love. This fear is clearly evident in the incidents of police violence against Black people. The police are trained to react to situations in prescribed ways, out of fear. Despite George Floyd's cries, Officer Chauvin, whose knee was on Mr. Floyd's neck, was unaware that a human being was dying beneath him. The video recorded by a bystander shows that fear had also frozen the other officers. They stood in positions of reaction, protecting their fellow officer rather than hearing the voice of a dying man. Clearly, they had never been trained that Black lives matter. Unaware, they did not see that Mr. Floyd's life was precious. They were unable to recognize that Black lives have inherent value and deserve to be cherished.

Their inaction contributed to our world's current breathlessness. But in response, we finally began to see one another. I also began to be aware. I woke up from my numbness. I began to come alive in new ways.

### The Habit of Awareness

I came to understand that I could not disconnect social awareness from spiritual awareness. The two are interwoven, inseparable. Awareness is the foundation of our spiritual lives. It is the first step in Ignatius's daily Examen, and it is equally necessary for any kind of meditation, the state of mind where we step outside our egos. We need to be aware of our sin before we can be open to God's unconditional grace.

The Ignatian Examen is a powerful tool for cultivating racial awareness. In the Examen, Ignatius invites us to do only one thing: make time each day to sit down with the events of our daily lives: review our day; analyze the data; ask God to help us understand what happened during the day—the hidden motivations and emotional reactions that lay behind our actions—and then be open to receive the grace for tomorrow's action. The Examen is not intended to be a guilt-inducing exercise but rather a way to become more self-aware, while turning to the future with renewed hope and energy.

The Examen asks that we make awareness a daily habit. In the process, we come to know what holds us back from acting in love. Unaware, we tend to focus on external success rather than internal healing. We fail to see the effects our actions have on others.

### Awareness and the Ego

A lack of awareness allows our egos to run the show and ignore the needs of others. The ego is like a shadow that blocks the sun of awareness. It makes us blind to the reality of injustice that is around us; we cannot see its presence because we are too wrapped up in our own concerns. Human selfishness prompts us to react in our own defense, rather than act in love.

Accusations of racism are a threat to white people's egos, their sense of who they are. This is what made my friend insist that he was not racist, and this is what made him walk away from me. As Austin Channing Brown has noted:

> White people desperately want to believe that only the lonely, isolated "whites only" club members are racist. This is why the word racist offends "nice white people" so deeply. It challenges their self-identification as good people. Sadly, most white people are more worried about being called racist than about whether or not their actions are in fact racist or harmful.[2]

Awareness shines a light into the ego's shadow. Or, to put it another way, awareness helps empty our hearts of their preoccupation with our own selfish concerns. As Father William Breault once wrote,

---

[2] Austin Channing Brown, *I'm Still Here: Black Dignity in a World Made for Whiteness* (New York: Convergent Books, 2018), 17.

"A cup must be empty before it can be filled. . . . In order to fill anything, there must be a hollowed-out space . . . emptied of the false self and its endless demands."[3] Awareness makes room for God to breathe into us and through us, filling us with the divine compassion that will naturally flow from us out into the world.

This is the starting point of any form of psychological, spiritual, or societal healing. If we lack awareness, we cannot discover the deeper truths beneath life's surface. With it, we discover ourselves in new ways. We allow God to confront us. We experience a breathing, living connection between the body and the soul. Ultimately, if we lack awareness, we lack God, for there is no room for God when our egos are so inflated that they take up all the space in our thoughts and hearts. With awareness, however, we can begin to grow spiritually—and in doing so, we discover that Christ is calling us to acts of justice.

This wide-awake, fully aware spirituality doesn't ask us to be reactionary, nor does it allow us to deny reality and become defensive to protect ourselves from it. Instead, this spirituality calls us to be active agents who can respond, be present, and enter into communion with God and others. We learn to be intentional with our actions as much as our words. As we ourselves begin to heal, we are empowered to work for the world's healing.

Caution is necessary, for the selfish ego can all too easily creep into our thoughts and actions. We cannot engage in antiracist work to impress our friends, nor should we set ourselves up to "save" people of color. As the great psychoanalyst Carl Jung wrote, "We should not use the other for our own supposed redemption. The other is no stepping stone for our feet."[4] We must be vigilant against the ego's demands, so that we care more about the dignity of our sisters and brothers than we do our own reputations.

---

[3] William Breault, SJ, in *Hearts on Fire: Praying with Jesuits*, ed. Michael Harter, SJ (St. Louis, MO: Institute of Jesuit Sources, 1993), 74.

[4] Carl Jung, *The Red Book*, ed. S. Shamdasani, trans. M. Kyburz, J. Peck, and S. Shamdasani (New York: W. W. Norton, 2009), 338.

### An Ongoing Process

Spiritual awareness is not a one-time event; it must be ongoing, a lived process that operates both internally and externally. Ignatian discernment is an ideal tool for keeping our awareness sharp and awake.

When Ignatius was convalescing after his injury, no longer able to participate in active society, he had no choice but to become more aware of his interior thoughts and feelings; as he did so, he noticed two contrary forces within him. The one that empowered him, giving him greater energy, he called consolation. The opposing force left him feeling restless and empty; he called this one desolation. As he thought about these interior feelings, he came to believe that consolation usually comes from the Spirit of God touching our hearts and thoughts, while the sense of desolation comes from the enemy of humanity's divine nature, what he referred to as the "evil one." Ignatian discernment is the process of awareness that comes from identifying these two movements within the soul. Although discernment is often applied to the decision-making process, it can also be used to heighten our awareness of the reality of societal racism, and to use that awareness to spur us to action.

As part of the continual movement of awareness, Ignatius calls us as well to pray for one another. In doing so, we rob the ego of some of its power over us. We remember that all of us, ourselves included, are still developing and learning.

This frees us to love each other more deeply. We recognize our common frailty as human beings. The Jesuit brother who doubted my ability to become a good Jesuit, is a white male who grew up in a big, industrial state in the Midwest; he also happens to be a Jesuit. I am a Black, Haitian-born male; I also happen to be a Jesuit. Both of us have had the grace to receive the Ignatian experience. While we are constantly praying, asking God for the grace to convert us on a daily basis, this doesn't stop either my brother or myself from being imperfect humans. Being human, we must always wrestle with our egos. Humility requires that I see this in myself as much as I see it in my brother. We are both deeply loved by God—and we are both in need of healing.

Without this awareness, the divisions between us grow wider and deeper; with it, we learn to see a larger picture, a deeper reality. We realize that our individual identities are wrapped up with one another. When faith becomes sight, we are empowered to see Christ in others.

We stop focusing so much on who is responsible for the suffering of Black people, and begin to ask ourselves, "What is keeping the cycle of injustice alive?" From this perspective, we can examine the institutions within our nation that motivate the killing of Black people. What is it that causes so many white people to perceive all Black people as criminals? Questions like these arise out of awareness—and out of awareness, we can begin to build a new narrative about being human and Black.

Awareness leads to action. In my own life, I sense the Breath of the Spirit around me, pushing me to take steps toward racial healing. Opportunities arise. Aware that everything I have is a gift from God, I experience a deep sense of gratitude. I am reminded that each of us exists for others.

Ignatian spirituality calls us to communal awareness. This allows us to look beyond the hyper-individualism prevalent in our world and see the bigger picture of our lives in connection with others. As we become aware of others, we recognize ourselves in them. We experience our common existence, and we can become a part of each other's lives. Freedom becomes something that is interconnected with each other. We create a reality where racism can no longer grow strong.

As Father Erich Rutten preached after George Floyd's death, in order to get past racism, "We need to get out of our comfort zones and encounter one another."[5] Together, in community, we can begin to breathe.

---

[5] Quoted by Christine Rousselle, "Christ Can Overcome Racism, Minnesota Priest Says at George Floyd Prayer Service," *Catholic Spirit,* May 30, 2020, https://thecatholicspirit.com.

**Invitation to Discernment**

Being aware is not easy. It requires daily effort. The following Examen[6] is intended to be used as a tool to cultivate the awareness required in the struggle against racism.

*Become aware of the presence of God.* Think about the God of the oppressed. Reflect on the marginalized of today's society. Whom do you see in your mind's eye? Remember God's love for them by seeing them. Notice any sense you may have that God's love is calling you to resist the systems, thoughts, and institutions that seek to prevent love and community. Remember there is no room for racism in love. Reflect on the systems that seek to keep us from loving one another. Find God in all things and all people—especially those people racism separates from us through hate, discrimination, and systemic oppression.

*Review how white privilege has affected your life.* Often we fail to recognize how the choices we make—both big and small—all contribute to a larger picture. Take a moment to ask yourself:

- What are the consequences of my decisions?
- How have my actions and attitudes allowed me to remain unaware of the true cost of racism?
- Have I listened when others told me their experiences? Or did I argue, ignore, or interrupt?

*Notice your emotions.* As you think about the systemic racism in our society, do you feel shame, anger, discomfort, fear, or hatred? Are there prejudices you hold of which you are becoming aware? However uncomfortable you feel, sit with the discomfort.

---

[6] Portions of this Examen were adapted from Maddie Murphy's "An Examen for White Allies," *Ignatian Solidarity Network* (blog), June 3, 2020, https://ignatiansolidarity.net/blog/2020/06/03/an-examen-for-white-allies-2/.

Don't push your emotions away. You may want to jot down your thoughts and feelings. Journaling can be another useful tool in cultivating awareness.

***Look forward.*** Reflect on ways you can take action against racism. Are there social justice groups or organizations you can join or support? Are there books, articles, or other forms of media on race that you can turn to for education? Are there people in your life with whom you may need to have uncomfortable conversations? Be prepared to translate the spiritual work of awareness into concrete, physical actions. As Ignatius said, "Love is shown more in deeds than in words."[7]

### Prayer

*Wake me up Lord, so that the evil of racism*
*finds no home within me.*
*Keep watch over my heart, Lord,*
*and remove from me any barriers to your grace,*
*that may oppress and offend my brothers and sisters.*
*Fill my spirit, Lord, so that I may give*
*services of justice and peace.*
*Clear my mind, Lord, and use it for your glory.*
*And finally, remind us, Lord, that you said,*
*"Blessed are the peacemakers,*
*for they shall be called children of God."*
*Amen.*[8]

---

[7] Ignatius of Loyola, *The Spiritual Exercises of St. Ignatius*, trans. Louis J. Puhl (Westminster, MD: Newman Press, 1951), 101.

[8] This prayer is from "For the Love of One Another" (1989), a special message from the Bishops' Committee on Black Catholics of the National Conference of Catholic Bishops on the Occasion of the Tenth Anniversary of the Pastoral Letter, *Brothers and Sisters to Us*, the U.S. Catholic Bishops' Pastoral Letter on Racism (1979).

# 7

# Community

*The end is reconciliation; the end is redemption; the end is the creation of the beloved community. It is this type of spirit and this type of love that can transform opposers into friends. . . . It is an overflowing love which seeks nothing in return. It is the love of God working in the lives of men. This is the love that may well be the salvation of our civilization.*

— Martin Luther King, Jr.[1]

Early in my graduate-school research, my advisor sent me to work in a community clinic in the Democratic Republic of the Congo. The people I encountered there were suffering from years of war, a war that in large part was caused by the division and greed of Western industry. A single mother I worked with had been raped by a soldier. Everyone had their own story of hardship and pain.

---

[1] Martin Luther King, Jr., *I Have a Dream—Special Anniversary Edition: Writings and Speeches That Changed the World* (New York: HarperCollins, 2003), 22.

This was a difficult period of my life as I struggled to be of use to the women who came to the clinic. My days were long and challenging, and I often found myself exhausted, both physically and spiritually. Then one day, one of the women in the community called me. "Patrick, come here," she said. "We want to pray with you and receive you into the community."

At this point, I had been in the Congo for six months; I assumed I had already been accepted into the community.

"No," the woman told me. "You need to be seen and received by all of us. Everyone needs to see you, as we see God in you." Her words began to open in me a new space, a space where I came to understand the connection between being seen by others and being seen by God.

Other experiences I had in the Congo widened that space. I struggled with the heat, and at night, I would be so hot that I literally cried, soaking my sheets with sweat. Sometimes, my South African friend, Noah, would hear me moving about as I changed my sheets. "*Sawubona*," he would call to me from his room. "We see you." Of course, Noah did not literally see me, since he was in his own room as I was in mine, but I was comforted that he was naming my existence. We were connected by the same spiritual reality.

"*Yebo sawubona*," I learned to call back to Noah. These words mean, "Yes, I see you too." These simple phrases expressed our mutual awareness of each other existing within a shared community. Despite my difficulty acclimating to a different climate and demanding work, I *belonged*. The community supported me.

My experiences in the Congo taught me the importance of being seen. We need this in order to come into the full expression of our own identity. The Neo-Freudian Jacques Lacan described an infant's sense of sight as the first witness to her own existence, while at the same time, through sight, the infant is invited into relationship with the world around her; it is only through seeing and being seen by others that the infant develops a sense of "I."

Lacan spoke of this as the "mirror stage" and concluded that ultimately we are who we are only in relation to other people.[2]

### Communal vs. Individual Identity

This is an idea that Africans seem to grasp intuitively. In fact, most African languages have a word for it: *ubuntu*, a word that has roots in many African languages. It has been translated, "I am because we are"; in Zulu, it is defined as *umuntu ngumuntu ngabantu* ("a person is a person through other persons"). Barack Obama defined *ubuntu* as the "recognition that we are all bound together in ways that can be invisible to the eye; that there is a oneness to humanity; that we achieve ourselves by sharing ourselves with others, and caring for those around us."[3] And Nelson Mandela, the great South African anti-apartheid leader, summarized the meaning of *ubuntu* as "the profound sense that we are human only through the humanity of others; that if we are to accomplish anything in this world, it will in equal measure be due to the work and achievements of others."[4]

The concept that community is essential to individual identity is still integral to the African American community—but it is in direct opposition to Western culture, which stresses the individual. This societal preoccupation with our own individual interests allows us to feel justified in focusing on our egos' selfish concerns. It doesn't take into consideration the consequences that our choices have on others. (For example, during the COVID-19 pandemic, many people felt that being asked to wear a mask was a violation of their personal rights.) Through rampant

---

[2] Jacques Lacan, "The Mirror Stage," in *Écrits: The First Complete Edition in English*, trans. Bruce Fink (New York: W. W. Norton, 2007).

[3] Barack Obama, speech given in Johannesburg, South Africa, at the Nelson Mandela annual lecture, July 17, 2018.

[4] See the preface by Nelson Mandela in Richard Stengel, *Mandela's Way: Fifteen Lessons on Life, Love, and Courage* (New York: Crown, 2009).

individualism, wrote sociologist Christopher Sofolo, "We can become so disconnected from others that our ethical imperative is destroyed and replaced with unabashed egoism. We become so obsessed with ourselves . . . that we disregard others at best and oppress and destroy them at worst."[5] And as Jesuit priest Michael Kirwan has noted, "Human individuals and communities are so convinced that they operate autonomously, and are so protective of this autonomy, that they are unaware of the violent measures to which they resort to maintain it."[6]

Awareness, which we discussed in the preceding chapter, is the necessary first step away from destructive individualism. As we become more aware, we realize that individualism is both a practical and spiritual fallacy. Physically, we human beings cannot exist without one another; we rely on both local and global communities for almost every aspect of our daily lives. By hurting others, we actually hurt ourselves, just as by helping others, we help ourselves. Spiritually, we are all interconnected; the Divine Spirit breathes through us all. We reach our fullest potential in connection with others. "We are all caught in an inescapable network of mutuality, tied in a single garment of identity," said Martin Luther King, Jr. "I can never be what I ought to be until you are what you ought to be."[7] This is the spirit of *ubuntu* that I discovered during my time in Africa.

This way of being, Archbishop Desmond Tutu wrote, is "the essence of being human. . . . You can't be human all by yourself." Tutu went on to note that such interconnection leads to the awareness that "what you do affects the whole World. When you do well, it spreads out; it is for the whole of humanity."[8]

---

[5] Christopher Sofolo, "Ubuntu and the Hopelessness of Individualism," *Sojourners,* April 25, 2012, https://sojo.net.

[6] Michael Kirwan, SJ, *Discovering Girard* (Lanham, MD: Rowan & Littlefield, 2005), 68.

[7] Martin Luther King, Jr., commencement address at Oberlin College, 1965.

[8] Desmond Tutu, *No Future Without Forgiveness* (New York: Image, 2000), 35.

*Ubuntu*, noted Tutu, leads naturally to acts of generosity. This practical, active, and interactive love also lies at the heart of Ignatian spirituality. Ignatius wrote in *The Spiritual Exercises*, "Love consists in an interchange."[9]

### The Beloved Community

The community of love and exchange was also essential to the teaching of Martin Luther King, Jr. His racial activism was directly tied to building what he referred to as the "Beloved Community." Each of his boycotts and marches, he wrote, had the ultimate goal of fostering and creating this community, a community based on "intergroup and interpersonal living" that transcended "our race, our tribe, our class, and our nation."[10] King's concept of the Beloved Community was based on the sacredness of each human being. "There is no graded scale of essential worth," he observed, "no divine right of one race which differs from the divine right of another. Every human being has etched in his personality the indelible stamp of the Creator."[11]

These ideas are upheld and expanded by Ignatian spirituality, where, according to the Jesuit author James Hanvey:

> The human person is never considered except in and through a nexus of relationships. We are never allowed to stand outside these relationships on our own; there is no sovereign self, exercising a contemplative grasp of the whole from some vantage point outside

---

[9] Ignatius of Loyola, *Spiritual Exercises of St. Ignatius Loyola*, trans. and ed. Elder Mullan, SJ (New York: P. J. Kenedy & Sons, 1914), 231.

[10] Quoted in John J. Ansbro, "Martin Luther King Held a Conviction," *New York Times*, January 19, 1986, https://www.nytimes.com.

[11] Martin Luther King, Jr., "The Ethical Demands of Integration," in *A Testament of Hope: The Essential Writings of Martin Luther King, Jr.*, ed. J. M. Washington (San Francisco: HarperCollins, 1991), 119.

> the material, historical and existential process of life. Indeed, it is part of the illusion of sin to think that we can exercise such independence. . . . It is a mark of our healing when we come to appreciate the truth of our dependence, our connectedness. . . . When I begin to understand and sense that this grace lives in all things, then I am ordered in a joyous self-emptying of loving service to the world.[12]

Ignatian thought affirms both the individual and the community. Within the community, we find our deepest identity—and at the same time, the community will function better when I am able to reach my full potential as an individual. I need the awareness to be myself in order to be able to enter into a relationship with my neighbor, while at the same time, the members of my community need to be well in order for me to be well.

Black people, with their spiritual roots still in the continent of Africa, have always understood the importance of community. We draw our strength from it. We celebrate it every time we gather for a barbecue in the park, eating the good food our mothers and grandmothers have cooked while we listen to the loud and happy rhythms of our music. We feel its presence when we join in song or prayer or protest. During my time in the motherland of Africa, I experienced this same spirit in the conversations between neighbors, in the visits to the tombs of ancestors, in spontaneous dances that lasted until three in the morning, and in countless occasions of laughter. I feel the presence of God in all these moments of connection.

When I was growing up, the connection between community and spirituality was woven through my daily life. In my household, each morning we went through the same routine: As

---

[12] James Hanvey, SJ, "Ignatius of Loyola: Theology as a Way of Living," *Thinking Faith*, July 30, 2010, https://www.thinkingfaith.org.

soon as we woke up, we would pray. We would also speak with the ancestors, the part of our community that lives on in eternity. After we had washed, we would say good morning to the rest of the family; I would kiss my parents and my siblings, and we would discuss the day ahead. Through the simple acts of praying, touching, and interacting, we engaged with our daily life.

### Community, Safety, and Freedom

Often, when a family member expressed some anxiety about the day ahead, my mother would say, "Go talk to God about this. Pray to see what Jesus will say to you about how you can be safe." Even as a rebellious kid, I learned to connect my personal safety with the community I experienced through my family's morning routine.

The sense of safety is an essential aspect of a healthy community. Blacks rely on their community for safety, but at the same time, they are constantly aware that when they step outside their community into "white spaces," they are no longer safe. Without safety, we cannot be free; our community is kept confined, forced to endure economic, educational, medical, and professional limitations, as well as threats to our physical safety.

Yes, slavery was abolished in the nineteenth century in most of the world's nations, but we are not truly free as long as we are not safe. Safety would mean that as a Black man I would no longer have to be afraid of being stopped by police while I am driving—but safety is also about improving and mobilizing resources so that everyone benefits from them, including people of color.

By restricting the access to resources, the world builds barriers against its own children. It makes them live in fear. It denies them freedom—and according to Martin Luther King, Jr., the Beloved Community can arise only in an environment of freedom. "A denial of freedom," King explained, "is a denial of life itself."[13]

---

[13] Martin Luther King, Jr., "The Ethical Demands of Integration," 118.

This is a loss of life on all levels, psychological as well as physical. Connecting the political and the psychological, Frantz Fanon refers to the "pathologies of liberty" that racism causes individuals in the Black community.[14] Economic equality and spiritual health cannot be separated without a sense of dissonance, the guilt that Ignatius indicates is a signal that we are vulnerable to what he calls the "evil spirit" entering our lives.

This is only one reason that the loss of safety for Blacks wounds the entire human community. A healthy community needs all its members to thrive. When some of us are held back from our full potential, we are all held back. As United Nations Secretary-General António Guterres said, "In an interconnected world, none of us is safe until all of us are safe."[15] Mr. Guterres was speaking of the battle against COVID-19, but his words apply equally to the crisis of racism.

As the pandemic forced so much of life to come to a standstill, we had the opportunity to become aware in new ways. Many of us were isolated from others, causing us to realize that we are social creatures, fueled by our interactions with one another. Our foundational sense of community was threatened, but in response, we found new ways to connect through technology. As we experienced the Age of Breath so intensely, we were also offered the opportunity to think in new ways about the role justice plays in human life. We began to see that when we deny justice, we sever the community. We realized that it was not only the quarantine that separated us. We are all under the threat of racial injustice. None of us is protected.

Meanwhile, the Black community shouldered more than its share of the pandemic's danger. According to research done at Johns Hopkins University, Blacks were infected with the novel coronavirus at nearly three times the rate of whites; Blacks were

---

[14] Frantz Fanon, *The Wretched of the Earth* (London: Penguin, 1990).

[15] António Guterres, speech given to the European Union, Brussels, May 4, 2020, https://news.un.org.

also twice as likely to die from the virus.[16] The racial disparity among essential workers was one reason why so many Blacks contracted the virus; research has shown that Blacks were nearly three times more likely than whites to work in health-care support roles such as nursing assistants or orderlies; they were twice as likely to work in transportation jobs such as bus drivers, movers, and taxi drivers; and they were also more likely to serve in seven other occupations deemed "essential" during the pandemic.[17] The entire community, both Black and white, benefited from Black labor, but Blacks were the ones who bore the cost. And then, to make matters worse, when Blacks were sick with COVID-19, the medical care they received was not equivalent to that which whites received.[18] As much as Mr. Floyd's death, these disparities reveal the harsh reality of systemic racism.

## The Challenge of Community

Now, as the world works to recover from the pandemic, we have the opportunity to build a new society—politically, ecologically, socially, and spiritually. We must ask ourselves: *How can we rebuild together? How can we become a healthier community where no one is denied the privileges of freedom? How can we begin to live out the spirit of* ubuntu, *so that no one is invisible and all are seen?*

Martin Luther King, Jr., believed that the creation of the Beloved Community depends on the "recognition of the solidar-

---

[16] Stephanie Soucheray, "US Blacks 3 Times More Likely Than Whites to Get COVID-19," *CIDRAP News* (Center for Infectious Disease Research and Policy), August 14, 2020, https://www.cidrap.umn.edu.

[17] Jeff Lagasse, "COVID-19 Deaths among Black Essential Workers Linked to Racial Disparities," *Healthcare Finance*, September 11, 2020, https://www.healthcarefinancenews.com.

[18] Michael A. Fletcher, "Black Americans See a Health Care System Infected by Racism," *National Geographic*, October 16, 2020, https://www.healthcarefinancenews.com.

ity of the human family."[19] Although there will always be differences in communities, the similarities between us must not only be acknowledged but also celebrated. We need to begin to *see* each other as we really are.

Living our lives with one another is also a fundamental way that Ignatius invites us to meet God. We ask ourselves daily: *How do I need to live in order for all to be free?* As we work to find the answers to that question, we draw closer, both to each other and to God. As we participate in each other's lives, the community as a whole grows stronger.

Today, the people of color are still waiting to be welcomed and accepted. In one of his homilies, Pope Francis reminded us that this is a "time of choosing."[20] Will we retreat away from the community, wrapping ourselves in a "me first" mentality? Ignatian spirituality asks us this same question. In his biography of Saint Ignatius, William Meissner states: "For him, it is on the basis of self-denial that the kingdom of God can be established. . . . Without a victory over self, there can be no rationality, no belief, no salvation."[21] Will we continue to allow our egos to rule our lives—or can we use this time to remember that we belong to a living, breathing body where all members are needed?

The Age of Breath is an opportunity to recalibrate and reevaluate the living web of relationships that supports us all. We are challenged to find ways to be in right relationship with those around us. This is where Ignatian spirituality invites us to enter into that space where none of us looks alike, yet we are all, at least in part, living the same experiences, expressing similar desires, dreaming the same dreams for the future.

---

[19] Martin Luther King, Jr., "The Ethical Demands of Integration," in *A Testament of Hope: The Essential Writings of Martin Luther King, Jr.*, ed. J. M. Washington (San Francisco, CA: Harper Collins, 1991), 121.

[20] Pope Francis, "Extraordinary Moment of Prayer," *Libreria Editrice Vaticana,* March 27, 2020, http://www.vatican.va.

[21] W. W. Meissner, SJ, *Ignatius of Loyola: The Psychology of a Saint* (New Haven, CT: Yale University Press, 2009), 88.

**Community and God**

In the struggle for a just community, Father Bryan Massingale, a professor of theology at Fordham University and an important Ignatian voice for racial justice, challenges us to look deeper than politics and society, into our souls. "At its deepest level," he affirms, "racism is a soul sickness." He goes on to say:

> It is a profound warping of the human spirit that enables human beings to create communities of callous indifference toward their darker sisters and brothers. Stripped to its core, racism is that disturbing interior disease that enables people to not care for those who don't look like them . . . policy alone cannot heal these wounds. Nor can we redress white nationalism and white supremacy through legislation alone. These evils require responses that engage the soul. This is the essential contribution that our faith can make.[22]

Ignatius taught that if we want to reform the world, we must first begin with ourselves. A community is only as healthy as its members. In my own life, I have come to recognize that my spirituality—my connection to God—depends on my recognizing myself first and foremost as an agent of justice born to serve others. I find my fullest identity when I am seen by others and when I truly see them. Together, we form a community that is connected with practical, lived-out bonds of love.

"A great nation is a compassionate nation," said Martin Luther King, Jr. "No individual or nation can be great if it does not have a concern for the least of these."[23] When speaking of the

---

[22] Bryan Massingale, "To Dismantle Racism, We Must Heal the Human Spirit," *US Catholic,* January 17, 2019, https://uscatholic.org.

[23] Martin Luther King, Jr., *Where Do We Go from Here: Chaos or Community?* (Boston, MA: Beacon Press, 2010), 188.

Jesuit work against racism, Father Pedro Arrupe affirmed that it "will be effective only to the extent that it is transfused with the spirit of Him who said: '*By this will all men know that you are my disciples, if you have love, one for another.*'"[24]

A lived experience of community is the antidote for racism—and the loving compassion that leads to reconciliation is both the foundation and the goal of that community.

### Invitation to Discernment

***Become aware.*** As you begin this Examen, take a moment to quiet your mind and heart. Notice what emotions you have been experiencing and what has triggered these emotions. Release these emotions as you exhale. Then focus your attention on God. As you inhale, allow yourself to feel the Breath of God entering you.

***Review your life.*** The communities you occupy are often a matter of choice. Ask yourself:

- Do I choose to spend my time with people who look like me, who come from the same background as me? Or do I find ways to spend time with those who at first glance may seem different from me?

Father Greg Boyle has said, "Human beings can't demonize people they know. Put enemies together, say, baking bread, and humans can't sustain animosity."[25] We can't really see each other if we are never close to each other. Closeness dispels ignorance and blindness, while a common cause can unite us in ways that reach past our differences.

---

[24] Pedro Arrupe, SJ, *Selected Letters and Addresses: Justice with Faith Today*, ed. Jerome Aixala (Brighton, MA: Institute of Jesuit Sources, 1980), 26.

[25] Sean Salai, SJ, "Saving Gang Members from the Street? Q&A with Father Greg Boyle, S.J." *America Magazine*, August 20, 2014, https://www.americamagazine.org.

***Look forward.*** Consider seeking out ways to work for justice with people who are different from you. What are three practical steps you could take in the next week? Ask for God's guidance.

**Prayer**

*Lord Christ, help me to see what it is*
*that joins us together, not what separates us.*
*For when I see only what it is that makes us different,*
*I too often become aware of what is "wrong" with others,*
*interpreting their actions as flowing from malice or hatred*
*rather than fear.*
*Even when confronted with evil, Lord,*
*you forgave and sacrificed yourself.*
*Teach us to do the same.*[26]

---

[26] Adapted from William Breault, SJ, "A Prayer of Reconciliation," in *Hearts on Fire: Praying with Jesuits*, ed. Michael Harter, SJ (St. Louis, MO: Institute of Jesuit Sources, 1993), 27.

# 8

# Compassion and Reconciliation

*Compassion is . . . the capacity for feeling what it is like to live inside somebody else's skin. It is the knowledge that there can never really be any peace and joy for me until there is peace and joy finally for you too.*

— Frederick Buechner,
*Wishful Thinking: A Seeker's ABC*

*In the end, reconciliation is a spiritual process, which requires more than just a legal framework. It has to happen in the hearts and minds of people.*

— Nelson Mandela,
*Notes to the Future: Words of Wisdom*

A missionary once received a Xhosan pipe, called an *inqawe,* as a gift. The missionary placed the pipe on a shelf and forgot about it. He did not understand that, for the Xhosan people, the pipe was meant to be shared and passed on to others. In the missionary's hands, it became an inanimate artifact, rather than a living practice that connected people to the ancestors and to one another. The pipe was meant to use the breath to build relationship and interconnection. By bringing people together, it was a vehicle for reconciliation.

Western culture tends to think of reconciliation as an act that can be done once and for all, like a peace treaty that is signed on a specific date and then continues to stand. Ignatian spirituality, however, sees reconciliation as an ongoing force that gathers momentum as it moves through groups of people. Without that active vitality, it will soon cease to exist. Like the Xhosan pipe, unless it is part of an ongoing practice, it will become lifeless.

### The Ministry of Reconciliation

Saint Paul taught that God has given all of us the "ministry of reconciliation" (2 Cor 5:18). The work of bringing people together lies at the heart of Ignatius's teachings. He taught that central to this work is solidarity—the healing of division—with those who live on the margins of our world.

Ignatian spirituality acknowledges that "ultimately, the roots of conflict lie in the divisions within the human heart."[1] Through the practice of the Examen, we seek to discover how God is inviting us to participate in the divine work of reconciliation.

In recent years, the Society of Jesus has focused on this work in its General Congregation. In 2017, the Congregation affirmed:

> [Ignatian spirituality] opposes the dynamics of violence, gathers us as Friends in the Lord, and calls us to love and serve in all things, together with so many other friends with whom we cooperate, we celebrate, we

[1] *Rowing into the Deep* (Rome, Italy: General Congregation 36 of the Society of Jesus, 2017), 32.

> communicate. Faced with huge challenges and even apparent failure, we still dare to dream of creating with them a different world because we know the One whose "power working in us can do infinitely more than we can ask or imagine" (Ephesians 3:20).[2]

Ignatius wrote that "God works and labors in all things created on the face of the earth."[3] In the words of the Jesuits' General Congregation 36, "We recognize the signs of God's work, of the great ministry of reconciliation God has begun in Christ, fulfilled in the Kingdom of justice, peace and the integrity of creation." The Congregation defined "faith, justice, and solidarity with the poor and the excluded as central elements of the mission of reconciliation," and it went on to say, "Rather than ask what we should do, we seek to understand how God invites us—and so many people of good will—to share in that great work."[4] Through participating in the ongoing work of reconciliation, we become companions with Jesus and co-workers with God (1 Cor 3:9).

As I was growing up, my parents were deeply involved in "church work"; they knew that they were co-workers with God, actively striving to create a more just world. As a preacher's son, I recognized that it was my job to also participate in this work—but I didn't really understand why. At first, it seemed like just one more chore, not that different from making my bed or sweeping the floor. I assumed I could engage in this ministry without ever taking the time to get to know the people I was supposedly working to help.

Then one day, my grandmother called me to sit and listen to the stories people told. She helped me understand that I needed to hear the voices of those who are suffering. "Justice," she told me, "is about compassion and vulnerability and empathy." As I learned to truly listen to what people had to say, I began to participate in

---

[2] *Rowing into the Deep*, 32.

[3] Ignatius of Loyola, *Spiritual Exercises*, 29, https://www.ccel.org.

[4] *Rowing into the Deep*, 14.

their lives in a new way. Without that connection, I eventually realized, social justice work is empty. No true reconciliation is possible without relationships that are built on empathy and compassion.

### Empathy and Compassion

As meditation expert Marshall Rosenberg noted, "Empathy is a respectful understanding of what others are experiencing. Empathy . . . calls upon us to empty our mind and listen to others with our whole being."[5] Ignatius taught the same principle, saying: "We should be slow to speak and patient in listening. . . . Our ears should be wide open to our neighbor."[6] And the great Buddhist teacher Thich Nhat Hanh has said that the work of reconciliation requires the art of "deep listening."[7]

Listening enables us to come close to others, to suffer alongside them and join in their pain. In fact, "suffering with" is the literal meaning of the word *compassion*, which comes from two Latin words: *com* ("with, together") and *pati* ("to suffer"). It is akin to the root meaning of *reconciliation:* "the act of bringing back together."

Compassion breaks down the illusion that we are separate; it brings us together. It allows us to recognize that our well-being is interconnected. It unites us in the process of reconciliation. As the great theoretical physicist Albert Einstein recognized, "A human being is a part of the whole." He went on to say:

> He experiences himself, his thoughts and feelings as something separated from the rest—a kind of optical delusion of his consciousness. This delusion is a kind of

---

[5] Marshall Rosenberg, "Culture of Empathy Builder," *Center for Building a Culture of Empathy*, http://cultureofempathy.com.

[6] Ignatius of Loyola, *Thoughts of St. Ignatius of Loyola from the Scintillae Ignatianae*, ed. Gabriel Hevenesi, trans. Alan G. McDougall (New York: Fordham University Press, 2006), 39.

[7] Thich Nhat Hanh, *For a Future to Be Possible* (Berkeley, CA: Parallax Press, 2008), 56.

> prison for us, restricting us to our personal desires and to affection for a few persons nearest to us. Our task must be to free ourselves from this prison by widening our circle of compassion to embrace all living creatures.[8]

The circumference of Einstein's "circle of compassion" is expanded by the awareness that Ignatius taught in the first step of his Examen. Compassion and empathy constitute another way to connect with the present moment and with those around us—in doing so, we make reconciliation possible.

This requires that we disconnect from the selfish aspect of ourselves that says, "Me first." "In compassion," said religious scholar Karen Armstrong, "when we feel with the other, we dethrone ourselves from the center of our world and we put another person there."[9] As we come close to others, we are more able to connect to our surroundings and to God. We are empowered to "rise above the clouds of ignorance, narrowness, and selfishness" that Booker T. Washington described in his autobiography.[10] From this new perspective, we can begin to heal the cracks that racism has made in our society.

We often think of empathy and compassion as synonyms, but researchers tend to define them differently. They categorize empathy as feeling-oriented and compassion as action-oriented. We may pride ourselves on our empathy for others, but it does the world little good if it is mere sentiment, if it doesn't move us to take positive action. "I don't want your love and light," activist Rachel Cargle stated, "if it doesn't come with solidarity and action. I have no interest in passive empathy."[11]

---

[8] Albert Einstein, letter quoted in the *New York Times,* March 29, 1972, https://www.nytimes.com.

[9] Karen Armstrong, "My Wish: The Charter for Compassion," TED Talk, February 2008, https://www.ted.com.

[10] Booker T. Washington, *The Story of My Life and Work* (Cincinnati, OH: W. H. Ferguson, 1900), 212.

[11] Rachel Cargle, quoted in Marc Bain, "A Black Adidas Designer

Psychologists and sociologists define empathy as "the ability to sense other people's emotions." People with empathy are able to imagine what someone else might be thinking or feeling. They recognize and understand another's suffering. Having empathy isn't always enough, though. It doesn't necessarily mean we'll do anything but feel bad. It doesn't mean we'll take action against suffering. In fact, because empathy can be painful, we may even avoid situations that trigger it. This is why some people avoid listening to the news; being exposed to the world's suffering is just too distressing. In the words of Dr. Tania Singer, a psychologist and neuroscientist:

> When I empathize with the suffering of others, I feel the pain of others; I am suffering myself. This can become so intense that it produces empathic distress in me and in the long run could lead to burnout and withdrawal. In contrast, if we feel compassion for someone else's suffering, we do not necessarily feel with their pain but we feel concern—a feeling of love and warmth.[12]

Dr. Singer went on to explain that the neural networks underlying empathy and compassion are very different. Empathy alone can cause us to withdraw, but when it is combined with compassion, it inspires us to form real-life connections with others. "We are not islands," Dr. Singer's research indicates, "but very closely interconnected by the linking of one person's affect directly to another's brain."[13]

---

Is Calling on the Company to Apologize for Its Complacency on Racism," *Quartz,* June 4, 2020, https://qz.com.

[12] Tania Singer, interview with the Cognitive Neuroscience Society, quoted in Sharon Salzberg, *Real Love: The Art of Mindful Connection* (New York: Flatiron Books, 2017), 215.

[13] Peter Fenwick, "The Neuroscience of Spirituality," Royal College of Psychiatrists, https://www.rcpsych.ac.uk/docs/default-source/members/sigs/spirituality-spsig/spirituality-special-interest-

Reconciliation not only takes place spiritually and socially but also in the very neurons of our brains.

Psychologist Paul Ekman, an expert on emotions, believes that empathy may be the foundation we need to understand that others are suffering, but that we cannot stop there. He defines "compassionate empathy" as not only understanding and feeling others' pain, but also being inspired to take action. Ekman says compassionate empathy springs from the knowledge that we're all connected.[14] This kind of compassionate empathy makes us reach out. It carries us from passive empathy to active compassion—and it is active compassion that can bring about reconciliation in practical ways.

Like reconciliation, compassionate empathy is not something that can happen in isolated incidents, nor can it come into existence overnight. Instead, like kindness and respect, it is a character trait that we must cultivate and then carry with us every day. It becomes the foundation of our connection with others, and it is the stimulus that spurs us to take action on behalf of others.

But how do we cultivate compassionate empathy? Ignatius of Loyola once again has the answer. Through practicing daily awareness, we open ourselves to the world's suffering. But we do not stop there. Instead, we allow the Breath of God to enter us and move us to action. "Love," said Ignatius, "ought to manifest itself in deeds."[15]

Dr. Singer's research supports what Ignatius already understood spiritually. She discovered that Buddhist monks, who regularly practiced meditating on others' pain—in other words, being aware of it at the deepest level—not only were known for their acts of compassion, but they also changed the neurological structure of their brains. The monks' meditation produced feelings that

---

group-publications-peter-fenwick-the-neuroscience-of-spirituality.pdf?sfvrsn=f5f9fed8_2, 3.

[14] Paul Ekman, *Moving Toward Global Compassion* (San Francisco: Paul Ekman Group, 2014).

[15] Ignatius of Loyola, *The Spiritual Exercises of St. Ignatius: A New Translation*, ed. John F. Thornton, trans. Louis. J. Puhl (New York: Vintage Books, 2000), 101.

are similar to a mother's when she hears her baby crying; no good mother would sit listening to her child cry while doing nothing. Dr. Singer's research made her wonder if other people could train their brains to shift empathy into compassion, and she found that yes, through practicing the same daily awareness the monks did, everyone can begin to change.[16]

### Compassion and Racial Reconciliation

The compassion that daily awareness engenders is honest. It not only makes us more truly aware of others, but it also allows us to see ourselves more clearly. We see the suffering of others, while at the same time, we perceive the places in our own hearts where we have allowed our egos to rule. Pseudo-compassion, however, holds itself separate and superior. It patronizes rather than identifies with those who are in pain. It gives itself a pat on the back rather than reaching out to others. It allows the ego to flourish.

Clear-eyed self-awareness and humility are essential to the compassionate work of racial reconciliation. As author Ijeoma Oluo has noted, "The beauty of anti-racism is that you don't have to pretend to be free of racism to be an anti-racist. Anti-racism is the commitment to fight racism wherever you find it, including in yourself. And it's the only way forward."[17]

If compassion is to lead to genuine reconciliation, it must also be all-inclusive. We must extend it not only to those who are in our own group or tribe but also to the entire human community. Researchers have found that humans are capable of feeling great empathy, even active compassionate empathy, for their own group, even while they dehumanize those who are not in their

---

[16] Fenwick, "The Neuroscience of Spirituality."

[17] Ijeoma Oluo, Twitter, July 14, 2019, https://twitter.com. Ms. Oluo is the author of *So You Want to Talk about Race* (New York: Basic Books, 2018).

group.[18] Ignatius's actions and teachings indicate that he believed in the dignity of each and every person, and today, Ignatian spirituality asks that we look past human divisions. We can no longer be white folks extending a compassionate hand only to other white folks or Blacks only taking action on behalf of other Blacks. We must begin to see all humanity as one family, one community, with no exceptions.

Father Arrupe wrote that dehumanization is at the root of systemic racism's social sin—but it is born in each of us individually when we allow ourselves to be ruled by the ego. He wrote:

> For by thus making egoism a way of life, we translate it, we objectify it, in social structures. Starting from our individual sins of egoism, we become exploiters of others, dehumanizing them and ourselves in the process, and hardening the process into a structure of society which may rightfully be called sin objectified. For it becomes hardened in ideas, institutions, impersonal and depersonalized organisms which now escape our direct control, a tyrannical power of destruction and self-destruction.[19]

### Spiritual Imagination

The dehumanization of racism—the inability to extend compassion to those who do not look like ourselves—can be countered with yet another Ignatian tool: spiritual imagination. In *The Spiritual Exercises*, Ignatius asks us to "enter into the

---

[18] Melike M. Fourie, Sivenesi Subramoney, and Pumla Gobodo-Madikizela, "A Less Attractive Feature of Empathy: Intergroup Empathy Bias," in *Empathy: An Evidence-based Interdisciplinary Perspective*, ed. Makiko Kondo (Rijeka, Croatia: InTech Open, 2017), https://www.intechopen.com.

[19] Pedro Arrupe, SJ, "Men and Women for Others," address made in Valencia, Spain, 1973, https://ignatiansolidarity.net.

vision of God." We imagine the love and compassion that God feels while looking at our world. As we see things from the divine perspective, we take on God's qualities of love, empathy, and compassion.

Merriam-Webster provides the following definitions for the word *imagination:* "the act or power of forming a mental image of something not present to the senses or never before wholly perceived in reality" and "the ability to confront and deal with a problem."[20] Both definitions speak to the power of the imagination to fuel us with compassionate empathy.

Spiritual imagination weaves together our physiological, spiritual, and psychological environments. It takes these three domains and combines them into an integrated vision. As we connect body, spirit, and mind, we are able to bring greater awareness and connection to the relationships we hold with ourselves, others, and God. We discover ways that our internal images and emotions can find expression in the outside world.

When I feel alone and isolated by racial discrimination, I picture my connection with those around me, even those who are physically distant, as well as those who may have hurt me. My imagination allows me to feel close to them. I feel a greater sense of community, and I experience the energy of compassion. Spiritual imagination has changed my life, helping to heal the broken self that was damaged by racial discrimination. I begin to see new ways to be in relationship with others. Everyone in the world is isolated in one way or another—but through spiritual imagination, we find ourselves in a compassionate community that strives for healing and reconciliation.

Imagination allows us to extend ourselves out beyond the narrow limits of our own lives. It enables us to connect with those whose lives have been very different from our own. It breaks the walls that shut us into our individual lonely lives and gives us insight into the experience of others. It can allow us to experience

---

[20] Merriam-Webster, https://www.merriam-webster.com.

compassionate connections, even when a pandemic forces us to quarantine ourselves physically. As it invites us to place ourselves in the shoes of another person, it becomes a tool of healing that helps us remember who we are and how we relate to those around us. By its power, we connect with the rest of the world, fueling a sense of wholeness that is no longer divided by race and tribe. The possibility of just reconciliation requires imagination.

Just as God gives us through mystical prayer the "explicit awareness that God is present and that the person clings lovingly to him,"[21] spiritual imagination is also a divine vehicle, through which God moves us to "desire the ineffable and unknowable."[22] By its light, we can see the invisible bonds that connect each person.

Without it, we are blind to the reality around us. Like my friend who insisted he did not see race, we fail to recognize the lived experience of those who live on the margins. Because something does not affect us directly, we say it does not exist. In her book *White Fragility*, author Robin DiAngelo describes an occasion when a white person said to her Black colleague:

> "I don't see race; I don't see you as black." Her colleague's response was: "Then how will you see racism?" He then explained to her that he was black, he was confident that she could see this, and that his race meant that he had a very different experience in life than she did. If she were ever going to understand or challenge racism, she would need to acknowledge this difference. Pretending that she did not notice that he was black was not helpful to him in any way, as it

---

[21] Harvey D. Egan, *Ignatius Loyola the Mystic* (Eugene, OR: Wipf and Stock, 2020), 23.

[22] William Johnston, ed., *The Cloud of Unknowing* (New York: Image, 1973), 81.

> denied his reality—indeed, it refused his reality—and kept hers insular and unchallenged. This pretense that she did not notice his race assumed that he was "just like her," and in so doing, she projected her reality onto him. For example, I feel welcome at work so you must too; I have never felt that my race mattered, so you must feel that yours doesn't either.[23]

When imagination is combined with humble, non-defensive listening, it can open our eyes to the reality of the other person. As we feel others' pain, we leave behind the I-don't-care attitude that allows injustice to thrive. No longer indifferent to the world's pain, we find ourselves inspired to take action, to speak out. Compassion and empathy become the foundation of our lives—and on this foundation we can build the work of reconciliation.

### The Courage to Be Compassionate

It can be tempting to want to run away from the fight. Whether we are Black or white, racism arouses painful emotions, emotions we might prefer to avoid. Ignatius, however, reminds us that if our emotions threaten to overwhelm us, we "should not withdraw from the company of others: for such movements are overcome, not by flight, but by resistance."[24] Using the vocabulary of psychoanalysis, Carl Jung also warned against avoiding negative emotions, saying, in effect, that if we run from suffering, we will in the process destroy a part of ourselves. He went on to say, "Only boldness can deliver from fear. And if the risk is not taken, the meaning of life is somehow violated."[25]

---

[23] Robin DiAngelo, *White Fragility: Why It's So Hard for White People to Talk about Racism* (Boston, MA: Beacon Press, 2018), 41–42.

[24] Ignatius of Loyola, *Thoughts of Ignatius of Loyola*, 48.

[25] Carl Jung, *Symbols of Transformation* (Princeton, NJ: Princeton

We can only find the answers our world needs as we work together. Whatever our racial identity, as human beings we are each called to the work of compassion, for this is the work that will bring justice to our world. Ignatian spirituality can support us in the long journey that leads us toward spiritual and social reconciliation.

### Invitation to Discernment

Angela Davis once said, "In a racist society it is not enough to be non-racist, we must be anti-racist."[26] In other words, for true reconciliation to happen, we must actively work to dismantle racism in our society. It is this same active approach that is part of Ignatian spirituality. The Examen that follows is intended as a tool to help you see more clearly how to be an antiracist who is working to build compassionate reconciliation in our world today.

***Become more aware*** *of the realities that people of color face.* One way to do this is to practice active listening; in other words, listen to understand rather than listen to respond and express your own opinions. Step out of your comfort zone by engaging in conversations that challenge the way you see the world. Don't assume you know or understand the experiences of marginalized communities. If people share their experiences with you, don't become defensive or argumentative. Instead, affirm and validate their experiences. Have the humility to be open to learning something new.

***Review your conversational and thinking habits*** *for unspoken stereotypes that can lead to microaggressions* (the brief statements or behaviors that, intentionally or not, communicate a negative message about people of color). Examples of this would be asking questions or making statements such as:

---

University Press, 1977), 110, 354.

[26] Quoted in Adam Rutherford, *How to Argue with a Racist* (New York: The Experiment, 2020), 201.

"What are you?"
"You are so well-spoken. You sound white."
"Can I touch your hair?"

***Get in touch with your emotional response to racism and antiracist work.*** Imagine yourself in situations that people of color face every day. Imagine that the life of a Black person is the lens through which you connect with God. Allow yourself to connect with the Divine through a Black life. What do you see? Who do you sit with? What do you smell? What is the color of the room or space you are in? What is the temperature? What voices or sounds are around you? Sit in this space for several moments. How does it make you feel?

As you allow yourself to experience the emotions that arise in you, begin to see yourself in people who are different from you. Notice any defensiveness, rationalizing, or reluctance you might feel as you do this exercise.

***Look forward.*** Plan how you can change your behaviors in the future and ask for divine assistance to listen and speak from a position of love.

Speak out against racism, including the microaggressions you witness. But don't try to speak on behalf of the person who has experienced the microaggression, since doing so can itself be a form of microaggression. "Having someone speak on their behalf can be unintentionally dehumanizing," says psychologist Kevin Nadal.[27] Speak from your own emotions rather than assuming you know how someone else feels.

[27] Quoted in Rebecca A. Clay, "Did You Really Just Say That?" *American Psychological Association* 48, no. 1 (2017): 46.

**Prayer**

Pray that you would be more open to the ongoing work of reconciliation:

*Teach me to listen, my caring God,*
*to those far from me—*
*the whisper of the hopeless,*
*the plea of the forgotten,*
*the cry of the anguished.*
*Teach me, Lord, to listen.*
*Amen.*[28]

[28] John Veltri, SJ, "Teach Me to Listen," in *Hearts on Fire: Praying with Jesuits* (St. Louis, MO: Institute of Jesuit Sources, 1993), 21.

# Part III

# THE SPIRITUAL EXERCISES

# 9

# Repentance

*Only when we come to understand, in the light of the Cross, the evil we are capable of, and have even been a part of, can we experience true remorse and true repentance.*

— Pope Francis[1]

*Ignatian spirituality . . . focuses not on coercing an individual to conform to rules and laws but coaches one on how best to open to God, who will lead one to freedom.*

— Sean Salai, SJ[2]

When I was growing up, my parents expected that, as a preacher's kid, I needed to be a model for the rest of the children my age. They took this very seriously, at a deep rather than

[1] Pope Francis, quoted by Nicole Winfield, "Pope Travels to North Sri Lanka, Urges Forgiveness," *Detroit News*, January 14, 2015, https://www.detroitnews.com.

[2] Sean Salai, "The Psychological Insights of St. Ignatius of Loyola," *America*, August 6, 2018, https://www.americamagazine.org.

surface level. Each day when I came home after school, the first question my mother would ask me was always, "How was your day with Christ?" She wanted me to never forget that Christ was always present in the everyday events of my life and in the people I encountered, and that I, too, brought Christ with me into every conversation and interaction.

As with most kids, I took this daily question for granted. I answered my mother automatically, without much thought. During this Age of Breath, however, my mother's question has come back to me. I find myself asking: *Where is Christ in the white, brown, and Black people who are so much at odds with one another? Where is Christ in the relationship between Black men and the police? As injustice ravages the nation, where is Christ?* Honestly, I do not have an answer to these questions. And yet I continue to ask them, knowing only that I am called to see Christ in my neighbor—and in myself. This awareness requires humility, a turning away from my selfish preoccupation with my own concerns. In return, I gain a deeper respect for myself, for others, and for Christ. These questions are at the heart of the first "week" of Ignatius's *Spiritual Exercises*.

### Unconditional Love

During this first phase of the Ignatian spiritual journey, the focus is on God's unconditional love, while at the same time we come to terms with our failures—and the failures of all humanity—to respond generously to that love. Ignatius invites us to review our sins, but we don't stop there. We see how God has always been with us, even when we weren't aware of the Divine Presence, even when we were living to please only our own selfish egos. Surprise often comes with joy when we discover that we are unconditionally loved. In Ignatius's language, we recognize that we are "lovable sinners."

To reach that point, Ignatius divided this first stage of *The Spiritual Exercises* into two major steps. We might be tempted to think that we should first examine our failures, before we focus on God's love, but Ignatius turned this around: first, we are invited to know who God is, and only then, second, do we recognize our failures, missteps, and brokenness as humans. With a better understanding of who God is, we now see that divine love is unlimited.

Through this two-step process that grounds our work in love, we enter into the history of humanity—a history of human depravity and the failure to love one another—with a clear recognition of the responsibility of who we are and who God calls us to become: people who are working for justice. This is both a negative and a positive spiritual experience. On the one hand, we gain a painful awareness of all the ways we have failed God and one another, but on the other hand, we come to realize the true essence of who we are in God's eyes. No matter how far astray we have wandered, we were each created for love.

### Systemic Sin

Sin—what the Bible defines as "missing the mark" (Rom 3:23)—can be personal, the result of our individual choices, but it can also be societal, which is so much more insidious and hard to recognize. Racism is a systemic sin. In one way or another, we are all embedded in it. In this first stage of *The Spiritual Exercises*, we are challenged to become more fully aware of our participation in a sinful societal system.

Systemic sin is not a modern phenomenon. As Louis M. Savary, an outstanding scholar of *The Spiritual Exercises*, notes:

> Jesus spent much of his public ministry stirring up awareness of some of the most hurtful social evils of his day, like religious hypocrisy among the priests and Pharisees, corrupt systems of justice perpetuated by the lawyers and scribes, unfair treatment of the poor by the rich, biased treatment of women, the social ostracism of

> tax collectors and the ritually impure, etc. Truly, Jesus bore the damaging effects of these social sins because he felt their evil impact daily on his own body and soul and on those around him. He had not contributed to these social sins or tolerated them, as we have. He was like us in all things but sin. Yet these evils were laid on him. They diminished him and his ability to convert people to a change of heart. What diminished him and the people were not only the personal sins of Caiaphas, Pilate, or Judas, but also, perhaps even more powerfully, the social evils of humanity.[3]

And so again I ask: *Where is Christ in the social evil of racism? How does racism diminish the Divine Presence in our world? How does it hinder the work of God, which is the work of justice and love?*

### Disordered Affections

The first section of the *Exercises* invites us to move away from egocentric thinking. We no longer put ourselves at the center of the world, and we let go of the attachments on which our egos grow fat and inflated. Instead, we learn to see others as part of who we are—and in doing so, we begin to heal.

Ignatius wanted *The Spiritual Exercises* to be an opportunity to recognize our "disordered affections," his terminology for what the Bible calls "missing the mark." Disordered affections are anything that keeps us from being free to participate in God's love. They are anything that has gotten out of balance within us, allowing us to place too much importance on some aspect of our lives, to the point that we give it priority over God and other human beings. This could be a job or status or material

---

[3] Louis M. Savary, *The New Spiritual Exercises: In the Spirit of Pierre Teilhard de Chardin* (Mahwah, NJ: Paulist Press, 2010), 63.

possessions. It might be money or food or social media. None of these things is bad in and of itself, which Ignatius understood. But our attachment to these things becomes "disordered" when we cling to them in an unhealthy way, allowing them to push God and others to one side.

In one of his homilies, Pope Francis referred to this same concept as "idols":

> We have to empty ourselves of the many small or great idols that we have and in which we take refuge, on which we often seek to base our security. They are idols that we sometimes keep well hidden; they can be ambition, a taste for success, placing ourselves at the center, the tendency to dominate others, the claim to be the sole masters of our lives, some sins to which we are bound, and many others. . . . Worshipping is stripping ourselves of our idols, even the most hidden ones, and choosing the Lord as the center, as the highway of our lives.[4]

### Repentance and Being

This situation calls for a complete conversion of mind and heart. It is what the Bible calls repentance: "Repent and turn around, so that your failures can be erased, in order that you can once more catch your breath from the presence of the Lord" (Acts 3:19; my trans.). Repentance sets us back on track, on the "highway" that is Christ—it brings freedom; it brings healing; it brings *breath*.

The Ignatian concept of repentance encourages us to face our way of *being* in three dimensions: how we choose to *be* with Christ, how we choose to *be* with one another, and how we choose to *be* (and in) our history.

---

[4] Pope Francis, Homily, April 14, 2013, http://www.vatican.va.

### Being with Christ

The first way of being brings me back to my mother's daily reminder: *How do I see Jesus in my life?* We cannot have a relationship with someone if we don't recognize their presence. Here, once again, we are faced with the spiritual importance of *awareness*. As we become aware of the Divine Presence, we interact with God as we go about our daily lives. This gives us a new understanding that the choices we make and our interactions with other people are all vitally significant, for they carry the potential of Christ's Presence. As we learn to *be* with Christ in this practical and everyday way, we re-center our conversations and relationships on Christ. We intentionally interact with each other in ways that connect us to God. This new awareness strikes at the societal racism that surrounds us. It asks us to see more clearly so we can disengage from a system that is deeply disordered (to use Ignatius's language), a system that leaves no room for the Presence of Christ.

### Being with Others

Racial justice becomes even more vital when we consider the second way of being: how we choose to *be* with others. As I think about this in my own life, I am reminded of a moment when I experienced both being in relationship and being excluded from relationship.

As Jesuits, one of the steps of our formation is to do a thirty-day pilgrimage. To do this, we are given $35 and a one-way bus ticket. The novice is then reliant fully on God and on the community of the city where he travels.[5] Ignatius instituted this

[5] This formative experience is rooted in our constitution, where it spells out that this "experience is to spend another month in making a pilgrimage without money, but begging from door to door at times, for the love of God our Lord in order to grow accustomed to discomfort in food and lodging. Thus too the candidate, through abandoning all

practice because he intended Jesuits to experience the discomfort of not knowing where they would sleep the next night or where their next meal would come from—and in doing so, gain a new awareness of God's grace.

In spring 2017, I did my pilgrimage. I left St. Paul, Minnesota, to embark on an unmapped journey that ultimately took me all the way to Key West, Florida. This was an experience that marked my formation as a Jesuit and changed me as a person. I learned to rely on God's grace in a way I had never before experienced, and I truly experienced the presence of Christ in others. But not every interaction I had during my journey was positive.

While I was in downtown Jacksonville, Florida, I spent most of the morning hanging out with people who were homeless. In the process, I made a good friend, Joe, who is still my friend to this day. When I began to feel hungry, I asked my new friend for directions to a soup kitchen where I could receive a meal. Joe gave me directions, and I set off walking.

When I reached the corner between St. Laura and Adam streets, I saw a woman walking toward me. By this time, I was very hungry, and I was anxious that I might miss the meal. Wanting to reassure myself that I was heading the right way, I approached the woman to ask directions. When I greeted her, however, she did not answer. Thinking she might not have heard me, I said hello again—and this time, instead of answering, she pulled out her phone and said, "I am going to call the police now and say that a Black man in blue jeans with a red t-shirt is asking me for my purse."

I was so shocked that I forgot all about my hunger. I turned around and went back to the park where I had left Joe. I made myself walk, but in my mind I was running. On high alert, I was

---

the reliance which he could have in money or other created things, may with genuine faith and intense love place his reliance entirely in his Creator and Lord." This is taken directly from the General Examen by Ignatius, no. 67.

constantly looking over my shoulder, afraid I would see police pursuing me. I was asking myself: *What am I going to do if I am stopped by the police? Should I run? Should I hide? If I let myself be arrested, will I be beaten, even killed?* If I noticed anyone looking at me, I wondered if the person was actually an undercover cop.

By the time I found Joe, I was shaking. I could not catch my breath. Although it was a hot day, I felt as if I were freezing. I did not eat at all that night, and my paranoia about the police made me decide to leave Jacksonville, rather than stay there longer as I had planned. To a white person, this may seem like an overreaction—but any Black person knows my fears were well-founded. They were based on the experiences of centuries of Black people. History has proven that it is not safe to be a Black person in white spaces.

My experience was very similar to the one that Christian Cooper had while he was birdwatching in Central Park when a white woman called the police, claiming that Mr. Cooper was threatening her life. Like me in Jacksonville, Mr. Cooper's only crime was being a Black person in a white space. The women in both incidents saw a Black man and reacted in fear. Their way of *being with others* was based on the perception of danger, rather than on seeing Christ in their brothers and sisters.

The events in Jacksonville made me realize that white people are more likely to perceive me as "other." Often, they cannot see their own reflection in my face. This faulty perception also blocks their vision of Christ. It makes relationship impossible. It leaves space for violence and hatred to grow.

In *The Spiritual Exercises*, Ignatius stresses the importance of entering into healthy relationship with each other, saying that for this to happen, "a mutual respect is necessary." Respect means that we focus on being open to the other's voice, "rather than a rejection of it out of hand." Ignatius counseled that our first choice should always be to put "a favorable interpretation" on others' statements, and any "confusion should be cleared up with Christian understanding . . . so that a more correct understanding may develop."[6] How might my day in Jacksonville—and Christian Cooper's in Central Park—have gone differently if the other person had employed Ignatian methods of interaction? Each time we intentionally change our way of being with others in order to reflect respect and a willingness to understand, we strike a blow to racism.

### Being in History

Finally, Ignatian teaching asks us to consider our way of *being* in light of history. As we look back at both our personal history and our society's, we cannot fail to recognize the privilege that some of us have and others do not—and yet arrogance and pride demands that we hide the ugly side of our history from our sight. Teaching children about racist history is considered by some to be "unpatriotic," as though love of country requires that we see through rose-tinted glasses.

This is a perspective that puts limits on love. It is contrary to the spirit of the first phase of *The Spiritual Exercises*, where we are empowered to look at our sins because we are secure in the knowledge that we are loved. As the Bible says, "There is no fear in love . . . for fear has to do with punishment, and whoever fears has not reached perfection in love" (1 John 4:18). The world's perpetual denial of racism has been motivated by fear. And when it comes to race, the more fear we have, the wider the gap becomes that separates us from each other.

Often, instead of accepting the challenge to *be* in light of history, we rationalize away the demands this would place on our life. We use arguments such as "*I* never owned a slave," or "*I* never enforced segregation." We insist that the past is irrelevant to our lives today, but in doing so, we deny the experience of the Black community. We make Black history invisible.

---

[6] David L. Fleming, *Draw Me into Your Friendship: The Spiritual Exercises. A Literal Translation and a Contemporary Reading* (Saint Louis, MO: The institute of Jesuit Sources, 1996), Annotation 22.

The way we live our lives today is shaped by the past. We cannot escape that truth. The great student of mysticism, Evelyn Underhill, also knew this truth:

> History will only be valuable to us in so far as we keep tight hold on its direct connection with the present, its immediate bearing on our own lives: and this we shall do only in so far as we realize the unity of all the higher experiences of [humankind].[7]

Ignatius taught that we need to see our lives from the perspective of what he called "good spirits" and "bad spirits." Good spirits are those that lead us closer to God—anything that helps create a realm of justice and love on earth—while bad spirits lead us in the opposite direction. As we look at the historical forces at work in our society, we need to ask ourselves: *In what way is the "bad spirit" of racism still at work in our world? And where do we find the "good spirit" that leads to antiracism? How can we join ourselves with that spirit? How can we disengage ourselves from the "bad spirit" of racism?*

These three Ignatian ways of *being*—with Christ, with the other, within history—are essential to the antiracist journey. As painful as we may find the process of becoming aware of what is "disordered" in our ways of being, it nevertheless takes us away from fear and moves us toward hope. Through greater awareness, we enter into community with others; we experience compassionate reconciliation. And in doing so, we refocus our attention on God.

### God in All Things

We cannot dismiss racism as irrelevant to our spirituality. For Ignatius, the most important aspect of spirituality is finding

---

[7] Evelyn Underhill, *The Life of the Spirit and the Life of Today* (New York: E. P. Dutton, 1922), 6.

God in all things. The attentiveness of the Examen leads to this awareness, especially the awareness of the presence of God in others. "God can and must be sought only within and through our human experience," wrote Evelyn Underhill.[8] Larry Culliford, a prominent figure in psychoanalysis and spirituality, emphasizes that at its core "spirituality is about wholeness." It requires that we rediscover "the essential qualities of indivisibility and non-separateness."[9] We are all interconnected with each other, with God, and with the spiritual world around us. Through the eyes of respect and love, we become for one another open doors into the Divine Presence.

Human life, however, is often such a blur of activity that we get distracted from the spiritual reality in which we live. We get so caught up in reaching our goals and finding success that we lose sight of the importance of wholeness and connectedness with one another. As we lose touch with God, we also lose our awareness of one another and of our own selves. We lose the perspective that makes antiracist work possible.

The first phase of *The Spiritual Exercises* calls us to become aware of the ways in which we have broken the sacred connections between ourselves and others. It challenges us to repent—and to *change*. As we move into the second phase of the *Exercises*, we will continue to be challenged as we are invited to focus ever more closely on the presence of Christ in the suffering of the Black community.

### Invitation to Discernment

In the Gospels, Jesus says, "The realm of God is close by. Repent and entrust your lives to my Good News" (Mark 1:15; my trans.). The Greek word for "repent" that's used in this verse

---

[8] Underhill, *The Life of the Spirit*, 8.

[9] Larry Culliford, *The Psychology of Spirituality* (New York: Jessica Kingsley, 2011), 32.

means "change of heart" or "turning around." When Jesus calls us to repent and entrust our lives to his Good News, he is calling us to turn our lives around so that they lead us to the "realm of God," the Good News that Jesus brought of love and justice for all humanity.

Ignatius taught that the Examen was a useful tool for turning our lives around. Through it, we can "speak to God as a friend speaks to his friend . . . now asking some favour, now acknowledging our faults and communicating to Him all that concerns us, our thoughts, our fears, our projects, our desires and in all things seeking His counsel."[10] We can accept the invitation to talk with God as we apply Ignatius's format to the work of antiracism.

***Give thanks to God.*** Consider the ways in which divine love is expressed through the work of antiracism. Become aware of your need for connection with other human beings. Open your heart to feeling gratitude for all the ways in which the Black community—and other communities of color—have enriched our world.

***Ask for grace to know your sins and rid yourself of them.*** Repentance is not achieved through our efforts alone; divine grace also plays a part. This requires an openness to God, allowing the Breath of Life to bring people, books, movies, and conversations to you that may help you realize more clearly the painful reality of racism, both in your own life and in society.

***Ask for an account of your soul,*** *hour by hour from the moment of rising from your bed, of your thoughts, words, and deeds.* Ignatius taught that this daily fine-toothed inspection of our thoughts, words, and deeds was necessary as a sort of strainer through which we could begin to remove the sin from our lives.

---

[10] Ignatius of Loyola, *A Thought from St Ignatius Loyola for Each Day of the Year,* ed. Melvin H. Waller, trans. Margaret A. Colton (West Monroe, LA: Saint Athanasius Press, 2010), 104.

We may easily dismiss this as unnecessarily extreme in today's busy world, but try making a practice of this for just one week. Pay attention to even the smallest ways—through your attitudes, through your conversations, and through your actions—that you participate in racism. Doing this for even a week will help to sensitize you to the reality of racism in your own life. You may be surprised by what you discover.

***Ask God for pardon for your faults.*** Racism is not only a sin against our sisters and brothers; it is also a sin against the Divine Presence that is found in each human being. When we participate in racism, we hurt the living God.

***Look forward.*** Resolve, with God's grace, to change the way you live. Once again, this is not work we have to do alone. We can pray daily for God's help and guidance as we commit ourselves to the work of justice and love.

**Prayer**

> *Let me not look away, O God, from any truth I should see. Even if it is difficult, let me face the reality in which I live. I do not want to live inside a cosseted dream, imagining I am the one who is always right, or believing only what I want to hear. Help me to see the world through other eyes, to listen to voices distant and different, to educate myself to the feelings of those with whom I think I have nothing in common. Break the shell of my indifference. Draw me out of my prejudices and show me your wide variety. Let me not look away.*[11]

---

[11] Steven Charleston, quoted in Rainey G. Dankel, Janis Pryor, Judith Lockhart Radtke, and Damon Syphers, eds., *The Anti-Racism Prayer Book* (Boston, MA: Trinity Church, 2014), 34.

# 10

# Identifying with Jesus

*We must hear the call of God in this time of crisis asking for us to . . . embody the very ministry of Jesus in our world . . . to be the body of Christ in the world, which means nothing less than showing up as Jesus did in his own day—in solidarity with the forgotten, outcasts, poor, and marginalized.*

— Kelly Brown Douglas,
"In This Kairos Time, Will We Embody Church?"

*Racism is the ultimate denial of the Gospel.*

— Desmond Tutu,
"Why, as Christians, We Must Oppose Racism"

Making friends was not easy for me when I first entered the Society of Jesus. I always felt like the stranger in the room, and in fact, some of my Jesuit brothers used that term to describe me: I was someone "strange," different from all the other white faces in the house. I shared meals with my brothers, went to Mass with them, exchanged polite words, but I felt little real connection. My "otherness" in my brothers' eyes prevented us from entering into a relationship of trust and intimacy.

Then, after I had been in the Society for about a year, I went on a road trip with one of the men from my house. We traveled from Highway 1 in Northern California all the way to Chicago, a journey that took us eight days. As we spent hours in the car together, we complained and laughed together. We had long conversations. I found myself opening up to him, while at the same time I sensed the dignity and respect he was extending to me. We chose to move past our differences and enter into a relationship of trust. As we shared the ordinary events of our travels, we found we could identify with each other in a way that had been impossible before. We became united by a friendship and love that continues to endure today.

### Intimacy with Christ

The second "week" of *The Spiritual Exercises* offers us the opportunity to enter into a new and more intimate relationship with Christ. We get to know him when he was a human being. As we contemplate his life, his light shines into the darkness of our hearts. We are illuminated, and with new eyes, we see the world more clearly.

Scripture tells us that in his birth as a human baby, Christ "emptied himself" in order to take on human flesh; he "did not consider equality with God something to be used to his own advantage" (Phil 2:6). This was a radical act of trust. Christ made himself completely vulnerable to humankind.

As Ignatius guides us to identify with Jesus's life on earth, we realize we have much in common with the man Jesus. He was not some alien being, different from ourselves, immune to the suffering of being human. As we spend time with him through the practices of Ignatian spirituality, we have an opportunity to go on a "road trip" with him, a time of closeness and shared experiences, just as I was able to have with my Jesuit brother. And as with me and my friend, we enter into a loving friendship with Jesus, a friendship that is based on trust.

## Spiritual Imagination and the Life of Jesus

Ignatian spirituality fosters this deeper relationship with Jesus in a couple of ways. The first is through our imagination (which we discussed earlier in chapter 8). As we read in the Gospels, the stories of Jesus's life, we place ourselves in the scene. We picture the smells, the sounds, the textures of the surroundings. We begin with the accounts of his birth and babyhood in the Gospels of Matthew and Luke, allowing ourselves to identify with Jesus's helplessness and innocence. We travel with him through his childhood and into his adulthood, as he faces the misunderstanding and oppression of his time.

Father David Fleming, an eminent Jesuit and a master of *The Spiritual Exercises*, refers to this as "imaginative prayer." He gives a good description of the way in which we can use this technique to come closer to Jesus:

> We become onlooker-participants and give full rein to our imagination. Jesus is speaking to a blind man at the side of the road. We feel the hot Mediterranean sun beating down. We smell the dust kicked up by the passersby. We feel the itchy clothing we're wearing, the sweat rolling down our brow, a rumble of hunger. . . . Above all we watch Jesus—the way he walks, his gestures, the look in his eyes, the expression on his face. We hear him speak the words that are recorded in the Gospel. We go on to imagine other words he might have spoken and other deeds he might have done. . . . Imaginative prayer makes the Jesus of

> the Gospels *our* Jesus. It helps us develop a unique and personal relationship with him. We watch Jesus' face. We listen to the way he speaks. We notice how people respond to him. These imaginative details bring us to know Jesus as more than a name or a historical figure in a book. He is a living person.[1]

### The Suffering of the Black Community

The second way we can enter into a deeper relationship with Jesus during this stage of *The Spiritual Exercises* is by relating Christ's suffering to the pain we see in the world around us. Instead of retreating into a life of comfort and privilege, we allow the suffering of others to become real to us. "Everything," wrote Ignatius, "has the potential of calling forth in us a deeper response to our life in God." As we take this to heart, we do not turn away from the reality of injustice in our world. We consciously choose to dethrone our egos from their place of authority in our lives—and, like Jesus, we "empty" ourselves; we stop grasping at our need to be important, to be better than others, to be free from discomfort. "Our only desire and one choice," wrote Ignatius, "should be this: I want and choose what better leads to God's deepening life in me."[2]

As we make this choice, we begin to see Jesus in the suffering of people of color. "God's presence in the world is best depicted through God's involvement in the struggle for justice," says religion professor Anthony Pinn. "God is so intimately connected to the community that suffers, that God becomes a part of that community."[3]

---

[1] David L. Fleming, SJ, *What Is Ignatian Spirituality?* (Chicago: Loyola, 2008), 57.

[2] Ignatius of Loyola, "The First Principle and Foundation," *Spiritual Exercises* [23], available online at https://www.bc.edu.

[3] Quoted in Barbara Bradley Hagarty, "A Closer Look at Black Liberation Theology," *NPR, All Things Considered*, March 18, 2008, https://www.npr.org.

As we become aware of the Divine Presence within the suffering of the Black community, we are challenged to affirm, "Black lives matter." And yet I have had friends counter this statement with the response that "all lives matter." Of course all lives matter; that should be a self-evident fact. But for centuries, Western society has been built around the assumption of white supremacy. We do not need to assert that "white lives matter," because no one has ever contradicted that fact. This is not to say that white people haven't suffered, particularly those who are poor, female, or at the margins of society in some other way; but they did not suffer simply because of the color of their skin in the way that Blacks and other people of color have suffered. For centuries, Blacks have had to face the constant struggle to assert that their lives *do matter*, equally as much as that of any white person.

The story of suffering is a long one. Historians often date the beginnings of racism to 1619, when a ship carrying captive Africans landed in a Virginia port. From this moment on, Black bodies were unfree bodies. They were not considered to be human in the same way that white people were.

But slavery and racism actually began even earlier than 1619. In the mid-fifteenth century, the treatment of "black Gentiles" was first addressed when Pope Nicholas V issued a series of edicts that granted Portugal the right to enslave sub-Saharan Africans. Church leaders insisted that slavery would Christianize the Africans' "barbarous" behavior, and so the pope issued a mandate to the Portuguese king, Alfonso V, giving him the right "to invade, search out, capture, vanquish, and subdue" the inhabitants of Africa and "reduce their persons to perpetual slavery."[4]

Although the Church at first limited African slave trading to Portugal, other European nations soon followed. The Netherlands, France, England, Portugal, Spain, Norway, and Denmark all participated. The supremacy of the white body over Black bodies

---

[4] Quoted in "Pope Nicholas V and the Portuguese Slave Trade," *Lowcountry Digital History Initiative*, https://ldhi.library.cofc.edu.

became a useful concept, an economically advantageous idea that allowed white men to grow rich. The world's growing capitalist economies were rooted in slavery, giving birth to the systemic racism that now spreads throughout so many social and economic structures.

As author Resmaa Menakem noted, racism grew up in North America, where "there is this shorthand that exists in the soil that says that [whites are] more human than [Blacks]." But then that belief was also exported back from the colonies to the parent countries. "So the progeny of the idea of the white body being the supreme standard has utility even in the parental countries."[5] These parent nations then carried the warped standard of white supremacy to all their colonies: to South Africa, to India, to Australia, and to other regions throughout the world.

Today, Blacks and other people of color around the globe continue to suffer twenty-first-century versions of slavery's suffering. Poverty, police brutality, mass incarceration, hate crimes, and unequal educational and professional opportunities are all aspects of that suffering. The second phase of *The Spiritual Exercises* calls us to open our eyes to these realities—and see Jesus present in the pain of the Black community.

## The Biblical Call to Justice

White Christianity has much to learn from the Black church. Five words have defined Black theology ever since the days of slavery: justice, liberation, hope, love, and suffering. The Bible echoes these same themes, and yet white Christianity has overlooked the calls for justice that are everywhere in both the Hebrew and Christian scriptures:

---

[5] Resmaa Menakem interview with the University of Arizona Center for Compassion Studies, https://compassioncenter.arizona.edu/podcast/resmaa-menakem. Menakem is also the author of *My Grandmother's Hands: Racialized Trauma and the Pathway to Mending Our Hearts and Bodies* (Las Vegas, NV: CRP, 2017).

> The LORD has anointed me; he has sent me to bring good news to the oppressed, to bind up the brokenhearted, to proclaim liberty to the captives. . . . For I the LORD love justice. (Isa 61:1, 8)

> "How long will you judge unjustly and show partiality to the wicked? Give justice to the weak and the orphan; maintain the right of the lowly and the destitute. Rescue the weak and the needy; deliver them from the hand of the wicked." (Ps 82:2–4)

> "Woe to you, scribes and Pharisees, hypocrites! For you . . . have neglected the weightier matters of the law: justice and mercy and faith." (Matt 23:23)

These verses related to justice are only a few of many, many more found in the Bible. And yet somehow white Christians have found ways to ignore these verses that are at the heart of their sacred scripture. Meanwhile, the Black church has read them and found a God who is on their side, a God who identifies with their suffering—a God who is with them. In the stories of the Hebrew slaves' exodus into freedom and Christ's suffering at the hands of his oppressors, Blacks found a God who no longer wore a white man's face.

### The Black Jesus

This is not an intellectual theology but one that has been lived and felt, one that has been physically experienced. It has empowered the Black community with hope. It has allowed them to look past the image of the blond-haired, blue-eyed Christ that was portrayed in so many white churches and see a Black Jesus—a Jesus who not only spoke out for the oppressed but who also experienced firsthand the suffering of an unjust system.

When we come into relationship with the Black Jesus, a man who was persecuted by the authorities, it is more than an intellectual exercise. Through the Ignatian concept of imaginative prayer, we identify with the suffering of Jesus within the Black community, and in doing so, we enter into a deeper intimacy with Christ.

And then we are challenged to go a step further. As we meet the Black Christ in others, we can no longer think of ourselves as "innocent bystanders" to the reality of racism. Once we allow ourselves to be truly present to the suffering of the Black community, we are called to take action. Christ calls us to embody his call for justice within our own lives. As theologian James Cone wrote:

> There can be no reconciliation with God unless the hungry are fed, the sick are healed, and justice is given to the poor. The justified person is at once the sanctified person, one who knows that his or her freedom is inseparable from the liberation of the weak and the helpless.[6]

The work of justice requires a wholehearted, active, and positive commitment to antiracism. There is no sitting on the fence, no neutral territory. Ibram Kendi pointed out, "One either allows racial inequities to persevere, as a racist, or confronts racial inequities, as an antiracist. . . . The claim of 'not racist" neutrality is a mask for racism."[7] This takes courage and a dedication to hearing the experience of others, while uncovering our own complicity with racism. It requires the humility to hear the stories of those who have been marginalized and excluded. Through the

---

[6] James H. Cone, *God of the Oppressed* (Maryknoll, NY: Orbis Books, 1997), 214. See also Elizabeth Palmer, "James Cone's Theology Is Easy to Like and Hard to Live," *Christian Century,* May 2, 2018, https://www.christiancentury.org.

[7] Ibram X. Kendi, *How to Be an Antiracist* (New York: Vintage, 2019), 9.

lens of Ignatian spirituality, we see God in others and at the same time we allow divine love to move through us.

The acknowledgment of the Divine Presence within the suffering of the Black community is not easy. It is not comfortable or pretty. And, as James Cone acknowledged, the reality of suffering can make us doubt the love of God. "How can one believe in God in the face of such horrendous suffering as slavery, segregation, and the lynching tree?" Cone asked. But then he affirms: "Under these circumstances, doubt is not a denial but an integral part of faith. It keeps faith from being sure of itself. But doubt does not have the final word. The final word is faith giving rise to hope."[8]

## Trust and Possibility

This brings us back to the importance of trust in both our relationship with Christ and in the work of antiracism. As the first "week" of *The Spiritual Exercises* stressed, God endlessly loves us and gives us life. "Our own response of love allows God's life to flow into us without limit," wrote Ignatius.[9] As my friend and I discovered on our long road trip, trust is what makes intimate relationship possible. It is what makes hope possible.

My Jesuit brother Greg Boyle has demonstrated the miracles that trust can achieve. In 1986, Father Boyle began Homeboy Industries as a ministry of trust and hope. At the time, violent police tactics and mass incarceration were considered the best way to deal with gang violence. But where others only saw criminals—many of them people of color—Father Boyle saw the face of Christ. He saw possibility.

His audacious trust in those who were considered to be untrustworthy looked like insanity. Even many of his fellow

---

[8] James H. Cone, *The Cross and the Lynching Tree* (Maryknoll, NY: Orbis Books, 2011), 106.

[9] Ignatius of Loyola, "The First Principle and Foundation," *Spiritual Exercises* [23].

Jesuits thought so. Today, though, Homeboy Industries is the largest gang intervention and rehabilitation program in the world. "Homeboy Industries," says Father Boyle, "has chosen to stand with the 'demonized' so that the demonizing will stop; it stands with the 'disposable' so that the day will come when we stop throwing people away."[10]

Racial healing requires trust. And this trust must be mutual. Even as we extend trust to others, we must be careful to be trustworthy ourselves. This atmosphere of trust is what Father Boyle has created through his work.

As a Black man, I have found that Ignatian spirituality prescribes trust as a spiritual medicine for the suffering of racism, even at the level of microaggression fatigue. Trust allows me to experience gratitude and forgiveness. I am not, of course, grateful for being exposed to a constant onslaught of microaggressions—but with awareness of the Divine Presence in each moment, I can be grateful that I have this opportunity to identify more fully with Jesus. I can allow the Breath of Life to move through me, rather than blocking its flow with resentment, defensiveness, or fear. I let go of the resistance that keeps me from inviting a broader perspective into my experience, and in doing so, I recognize that I live within a spiritual reality. My experience in this world is temporary, but God's love is eternal. With this knowledge, I have a renewed sense of peace, freedom to breathe, and hope. I can pray with Ignatius:

> Jesus, may all that is you flow into me. May your body and blood be my food and drink. May your passion and death be my strength and life. Jesus, with you by my side enough has been given. May the shelter I seek be the shadow of your cross. Let me not run from the love which you offer, but hold me safe from the forces

---

[10] Gregory Boyle, SJ, "Homeboy Industries: Producing Hope," *Huffpost,* September 8, 2009, https://www.huffpost.com.

> of evil. On each of my dyings shed your light and your love. Keep calling to me until that day comes, when with your saints, I may praise you forever. Amen.[11]

This second week of contemplation comes as a treasure and a challenge. It requires our constant attention to social injustice. It shines brightly during the Age of Breath, allowing us to meet Christ in the suffering of people of color. The powers of our imagination can inspire us to actively work toward peace and reconciliation.

The grace we seek during the second phase of *The Spiritual Exercises* is captured in a prayer that Ignatius included in *The Spiritual Exercises*, one that is often repeated by Jesuits: "Lord, grant that I may see thee more clearly, love thee more dearly, and follow thee more nearly." As we enter into this deeper, more intimate relationship of trust, we turn away from racial superiority, from greed and pride, and instead, we consciously choose to align ourselves with the spiritual poverty, self-emptying, and humility that leads to racial equity. We step away from fear and defensiveness, and we enter into new intimacy with both God and others. As we meet Christ in one another, we are empowered to risk going beyond our limitations. We become people of possibility.

Next, in the third "week" of the *Exercises*, we will focus on Christ's death on the cross—and in doing so, we will gain a still deeper insight into what it means to encounter God in the Age of Breath.

### Invitation to Discernment

Once again, we use the format of the Examen to help us encounter the Presence of Christ in all humanity.

---

[11] Ignatius of Loyola. This modern version of the prayer was developed by David L. Fleming, SJ, and can be found in *Hearts on Fire: Praying with Jesuits* (St. Louis, MO: Institute of Jesuit Sources, 1993), 7.

***Remind yourself that you are in God's presence.*** *Give thanks for God's love for all who have been made in the divine image.* Allow yourself to imagine what it would have been like to have been kidnapped from your home in Africa during the days when the slave trade flourished. Open your heart to the centuries of suffering the Black community has endured.

***Ask God to reveal to you how embedded racial assumptions might have shaped your attitudes and actions today.*** Take time to consider these questions:

- Have I done anything to diminish the image of God in people of color?
- Have I been silent when I could have spoken truth and love into a racist situation?
- Have I laughed at or participated in jokes that denigrated people of color?
- Do I blame the victims of poverty and oppression for their pain?
- Do I come up with excuses for things I have done or said that were perceived as racist by others?
- Do I take the time to learn and listen to the stories of others' lives in order to better understand them and the challenges they may face that I do not?
- Do I see Jesus in each and every person I encounter?

***Look forward.*** Open yourself, with God's help, to the call to be active in bringing peace and justice to the world around you. Prayerfully ask yourself:

- How can I extend the love of God to people of color with my words, deeds, actions, and influence?
- What action can I take tomorrow to actively express my longing for racial justice?
- How can I express my solidarity with all who have been marginalized? What practical action can I take?

- Where in my life do I see opportunities to establish relationships of trust, respect, and dignity with people of color?

**Prayer of Dedication**

Pray that the Jesus who lives in the suffering of all humanity might also live and love through you.

*Lord Jesus,*
*I give you my hands to do your work.*
*I give you my feet to follow your path.*
*I give you my eyes to see as you see.*
*I give you my tongue to speak your words.*
*I give you my mind so you can think in me.*
*I give you my spirit so you can pray in me.*
*Above all I give you my heart so in me you can love your Father and all people.*
*I give you my whole self so you can grow in me, till it is you who live and work and pray in me. Amen.*[12]

[12] *The Catholic Prayer Book*, ed. Msgr. Michael Buckley and Tony Castle (Cincinnati, OH: Servant Books, 2013), 188–89.

11

# The Crucifixion

*I'm tired of Jesus literally saying, "I can't breathe," on the streets of America while everyone turns their back on him.*

— Lenny Duncan[1]

*I believe that the cross placed alongside the lynching tree can help us to see Jesus in America in a new light, and thereby empower people who claim to follow him to take a stand against white supremacy and every kind of injustice.*

— James H. Cone,
*The Cross and the Lynching Tree*

I had waited to join the Society of Jesus for many years, and so, when the time finally came, I was filled with joy and anticipation. A dear friend of mine drove me to the novitiate in St. Paul, Min-

[1] Lenny Duncan, quoted in Isabella Rosario, "Jesus Was Divisive: A Black Pastor's Message to White Christians," *NPR*, June 12, 2020, https://www.npr.org.

nesota. The moment I arrived, I leapt out of the car and entered the building with a deep sense of both commitment and courage. My new life had finally begun. I literally danced with excitement, like a boy who has been given a marvelous gift.

But as time went by, my feelings changed. *I* changed. I realized what it means to be a Black man in America, and I began to look at life more seriously. A tectonic shift occurred within me. Meanwhile, my surroundings at the novitiate still looked exactly the same, but now it was as though they had changed color because I was looking at them through a different lens.

When I finally realized what was happening, it was a tipping point for me. Eventually, it would lead me to a new understanding of what it means to live by faith. But that was not an easy process. A part of me would have to die in order to accept a new reality. *The Spiritual Exercises*, especially the third stage, helped me process this experience.

### The Experience of Death

In the third "week" of *The Spiritual Exercises*, we focus on the death of Jesus. We meditate on what his death means to us—and what it asks of us. Jesuit David Fleming describes this phase of the *Exercises* as a time when we face our tendency to avoid pain:

> When we cannot change a situation, we are tempted to walk away from it. We might literally walk away; we are too busy to sit with a suffering friend. Or we walk away emotionally; we harden ourselves and maintain an emotional distance. We might react to the Gospel accounts of Jesus' passion and death this way. They describe something terrible and horribly painful, yet we might shield ourselves from the pain. We *know* the

story of the Passion. Ignatius wants us to *experience* it as something fresh and immediate. We learn to suffer with Jesus, and thus learn to suffer with the people in our lives.[2]

## Say Their Names

This willingness to be present to suffering calls us once again to see Jesus in the Black community—but now we will go still deeper. As we enter into Christ's experience on the cross, we feel his breathlessness. We gasp for oxygen. And then we realize that this is the same agony that George Floyd, Breonna Taylor, and many others experienced as they died. With Jesus, they cried out, "I can't breathe! Please hear me!" As we say the names of Black men and women killed by police, it becomes a litany of breath:

> John Crawford III, Michael Brown, Dante Parker, Michelle Cusseaux, Laquan McDonald, George Mann, Tanisha Anderson, Michael Brown, Akai Gurley, Tamir Rice, Rumain Brisbon, Jerome Reid, Matthew Ajibade, Alton Sterling, Frank Smart, Walter Scott, Natasha Mckenna, Tono Robinson, Anthony Hill, Mya Hall, Phillip White, Eric Harris, Walter Scott, William Chapman II, Alexia Christian, Breadon Glenn, Victor Manuel Larosa, Jonathan Sanders, Freddi Blue, Joseph Man, Salvador Ellswood, Sandra Bland, Albert Joseph Davis, Darrius Stewart, Billi Ray Davis, Samuel Dubose, Michael Sabbie, Brian Keith Day, Christian Taylor, Troy Robinson Asshams Pharaoh Manley, Botham Jean, Pamela Turner, Dominique Clayton, Atatiana Jefferson, Christopher Whitfield, Christopher McCorey, Ahmaud

[2] David L. Fleming, SJ, *What Is Ignatian Spirituality?* (Chicago: Loyola Press, 2008), 85.

> Arbery, Eric Reason, Michael Lorenzo Dean, Rayshard Brooks, Vincent Belmonte, Patrick Lynn Warren Sr., Andre Maurice Hill, Casey Christopher Goodson, Angelo Crooms, Sincere Pierce, Marcellis Stinnette, Eric Garner, Philando Castile . . .

The names do not end there; this is only a small portion of the litany of breath. Over the centuries, millions of Black women and men have died with the same plea on their lips: "O God of Justice, help us to breathe." And we can extend the litany as we remember the names of those who died through lynchings:

> Huie Conorly, Jack Mingo, Eliza Woods, Amos Miller, Orion Anderson, George Meadows, Joe Coe, Tom Moss, Calvin McDowell, Will Stewart, William Shorter, Charles Willis, Alfred Daniels, Frazier B. Baker, Sam Hose, Anderson Gause, Ed Johnson, Bunk Richardson, Slab Pitts, William Miller, David Walker (with his wife and four children), Jake Wades, Laura Nelson (and her fourteen-year-old son), Henry White, Allen Turner, Cordella Stevenson, Anthony Crawford, Mary Turner, Wilbur Little, Eugene Williams, Robert Robinson, Bob Ashley, Lemuel Walters, Lloyd Clay, Frank Livingston, Scott Henry, July Perry, Jesse Eley, Henry Lowry, John Parker, Elwood Higginbotham, Elbert Williams, Willie James Howard, Isadore Banks, Emmett Till, James Chaney, Frank Morris, Michael Donald, Willie Turks, Michael Griffith, James Byrd Jr. . . .

Between 1880 and 1998, whites lynched nearly five thousand Black men and women. This happened across the country, from the North to the South. Why were these men and women lynched? Why were they denied their breath? The reasons vary. One man was a waiter, who told a white woman that he needed a few moments before he could serve her; several men were killed for wearing their own World War II uniforms; many Black lynching victims had had consensual relationships with white women. Other reasons for lynchings were voting, owning a prosperous farm, asking for wages, teaching children to read, picking peaches from a neighbor's tree, starting an NAACP chapter, sending a Christmas card to a white girl, having too much money, being a civil rights worker, and driving or walking through a white neighborhood. Many times, the lynchings stemmed from rumor; and often they were carried out simply because a group of white men "felt like killing" a Black person. Lynching is no longer an accepted part of American life, the way it once was—but as a Black man, I still have to watch my step. It is still dangerous to be Black; events during the Age of Breath have proved that.

Racism not only makes Black people suffer. It kills them. Centuries after the arrival of the first slaves on America's shores, a century and a half after Blacks were emancipated from slavery, and more than five decades after the passage of the voting rights acts, the deaths continue. *The Spiritual Exercises* challenge us not to deny Blacks pain but to let it be our own pain. We are asked not only to say the names of those who were killed by racism but to imagine their faces, to understand that each individual had family and friends; each death was a loss of all that person might have contributed to the world. As we open ourselves to this pain, we hear the cry of a human Christ. We realize that racism puts Jesus to death all over again.

### The Cross and the Death of Black Bodies

In *The Cross and the Lynching Tree*, James Cone makes a direct connection between the crucifixion of Jesus and the unjust deaths of Black men and women. He writes:

> Until we can see the cross and the lynching tree together, until we can identify Christ with a "recrucified" black

> body hanging from a lynching tree, there can be no genuine understanding of Christian identity in America, and no deliverance from the brutal legacy of slavery and white supremacy.[3]

Martin Luther King, Jr., recognized the deep and painful connections between the cross of Jesus and the challenge to fight racism. "When I took up the cross," he wrote, "I recognized its meaning."[4] King knew that following Jesus into the struggle for justice has a cost, but he committed himself to that path.

Many followers of Christ do not take the cross seriously. They may wear it on necklaces; they place it prominently on their churches; but they have ceased to be aware of the challenge that the cross places on their lives. Imagine now—just for a moment—that Christ had been lynched instead of crucified. Picture wearing a tiny gold noose on a chain around your neck, or hanging a knotted rope at the front of every church. Such a sight would be shocking, horrifying. It would make us face the real brutality of Christ's death. It would allow us to see a Black Jesus whose life was all about bringing justice and hope—no matter the cost—to those whom society had pushed aside. The cross, said Martin Luther King, Jr., "is not something that you wear. The cross is something that you bear and ultimately that you die on."[5]

Western society doesn't like to think about death. We want life to be easy, convenient, and fast. But the Age of Breath has made us slow down. It's made life more difficult. It's given us the chance to reexamine our lives—and in doing so, we have the opportunity to realize that we cannot look away from the reality of racism.

---

[3] James H. Cone, *The Cross and the Lynching Tree* (Maryknoll, NY: Orbis Books, 2011), xv.

[4] Martin Luther King, Jr., quoted in Matthew C. Whitaker, *Peace Be Still: Modern Black America* (Lincoln: University of Nebraska Press, 2014), 128.

[5] Whitaker, *Peace Be Still*, 128.

## Constructive Guilt

Allowing ourselves to say the names of the Black women and men who have died because of racism—to experience this litany of breath—is not only painful; it can also make us feel the unpleasant emotion of guilt. Guilt is something else that most of us would rather avoid. But guilt is part of the human experience. As Carlos Domínguez-Morano, a Jesuit psychoanalyst, wrote, "The feeling of guilt is, indeed, one of the oldest, most archaic, and primitive human experiences."[6] Domínguez-Morano affirmed that guilt can be constructive. It redirects our attention away from external success so that we become more aware of our interior lives. It is a heavy feeling, but it can be necessary and beneficial. Domínguez-Morano went on to say that guilt is a necessary component of antiracism. "We need that psychic structure that will cause inner discomfort when our behavior strays from what we set as an ethical or religious ideal when we are talking about race."[7]

Psychoanalyst Frantz Fanon insisted that "white guilt" can do just the opposite: it can be a way for whites to stroke their egos by insisting on their commitment to antiracism while still avoiding the actual work of dismantling racism. According to Fanon, whites can indulge in a glorification of their own "suffering" as they contemplate the evils of racism.[8] But this is not the type of guilt that Father Domínguez-Morano described. Genuine guilt causes us pain, he said, because the ego is diminished by the acknowledgment of wrongdoing.

Jesuit author George Aschenbrenner explained that this is what it means to identify with the suffering of Christ: we turn

---

[6] Carlos Domínguez-Morano, SJ, *Belief after Freud: Religious Faith through the Crucible of Psychoanalysis* (New York: Routledge, 2018), 122.

[7] Domínguez-Morano, SJ, *Belief after Freud*, 125.

[8] Blake Smith, "Frantz Fanon and the American Racial Eros," *Tablet*, April 14, 2020, https://www.tabletmag.com.

away from our own feelings, so that we are freed through love to experience the pain of others:

> The focus is not on your suffering but on that of your beloved. A great emptiness of self and ego is required if this grace is to be effective. Such a grace is never easy, especially in our twenty-first-century American culture of self-absorption. . . . The consolation you seek comes from entering the suffering of Jesus. This ability to get out of your own suffering and to enter his teaches a very important lesson: to enter the suffering of other people you must get free of the all-absorbing clutches of your own.[9]

Instead of pulling away from the pain of guilt as quickly as possible, we need to embrace it and sit in the discomfort. This does not mean that we wallow in it, but rather that we have the courage to look squarely at the sin in our lives. We should not run away from conversations and information about race that cause us difficulty. We have to expect that they will be hard and painful. But out of this discomfort can come the impetus to work for change. This is what Ignatian spirituality calls for: an awareness of guilt that leads to positive action in the real world.

Domínguez-Morano emphasized that religion has too often abused guilt, making it unhealthy. Guilt, he wrote, can be based on "the danger of losing the love of the other, in this case, God."[10] He used the stories of Peter and Judas as examples of healthy and unhealthy guilt: guilt can drive us to transformation or self-destruction.[11] Ignatius addressed this in his teaching in the first

---

[9] George Aschenbrenner, SJ, *Stretched for Greater Glory: What to Expect from the Spiritual Exercises* (Chicago: Loyola Press, 2004), 122.

[10] Domínguez-Morano, SJ, *Belief after Freud*, 125.

[11] According to the gospel stories, Judas's guilt for his role in Christ's betrayal drove him to commit suicide, while Peter's guilt over

week of *The Spiritual Exercises*: we should experience our guilt, he said, within the context of divine love. We are never in danger of losing that love. Despite our brokenness, we are endlessly, utterly secure. As Jesuit author Gerald Fagin has written:

> We are sinners, but we are forgiven. The two are connected. Only when we claim our sinfulness and stand in sorrow before God can we truly experience God's mercy. We are loved sinners. God loves us even when we are sinners. Only when we know the depth of our sin do we know the depth of God's mercy. We are not as good as we thought, but we are much more loved than we ever imagined.[12]

### Prayerful Imagination

The prayerful imagination that Ignatius taught comes into play here once again. Through imagination, we allow ourselves to viscerally *feel* the pain of Christ on the cross, as well as the centuries-long pain of the Black community. But we do not stop there. We allow the imagination to open up new possibilities—and it is in the light of those possibilities that we can begin to change the world.

Personally, my lack of spiritual imagination during the Age of Breath led me into what Ignatius called "desolation," a state of self-obsessed depression during which I felt separated from God. The daily news triggered this pain, as I tried to repress my reactions to the violence and racial discrimination that were so prevalent.

During the Age of Breath, I heard Black people call white people racist, while whites called Blacks criminals. Indigenous

---

his betrayal of Christ inspired him to change his life and become the "rock" on which the Church was built.

[12] Gerald M. Fagin, SJ, *Discovering Your Dream: How Ignatian Spirituality Can Guide Your Life* (Chicago: Loyola Press, 2013).

people were calling white people colonizers; white people were calling indigenous people animals. Conservatives called liberals lib-tards, and liberals called conservatives extremists. We were embroiled in a sociology of name-calling, a vicious circle of pointing fingers. I could not imagine the possibility of healing.

But my spiritual desolation was self-imposed. Finally, I sat with the feeling and allowed myself to become aware of both my inner pain and the world's outer pain. Seeing my own racial wound was not easy. It was a dark place. But I had to go there so that I could begin to imagine the possibility of healing with my sisters and brothers.

### Releasing Attachment

Through identifying with the suffering of Christ, experienced through the suffering of others, we are challenged to let go of the ego, that selfish center point within us. This means, in more concrete terms, we release our tight grasp on our attachments. In Ignatian vocabulary, we become "indifferent."

We all have attachments: chocolate, football, music, a cellphone. Among my own many attachments is my blanket. Whether it is summer, fall, spring, or winter, I need my blanket. In fact, I even carry a blanket with me to my office. Now, obviously, there's nothing wrong with being attached to my blanket, just as there's nothing wrong with enjoying chocolate, football, music, or our cellphones. But, as we discussed in chapter 9, Ignatius taught that our attachments can become "disordered" when they make us blind to both God and others. They can become the defense mechanisms we use to justify our acts against creation. Our fear of losing these inanimate things can take away our freedom.

Ultimately, we often find we need to release our attachments in order to grow. When I first came to America, for example, I was attached to my idealized image of what I thought the Jesuits should be. Like my fondness for my blanket, this too was an innocent attachment—and yet I had to let it go before I could grow. When I finally did release it, I was free to enter into a new understanding of Christ, of myself, and of the Black community.

Psychologist Frantz Fanon viewed racial injustice as the result of an unhealthy attachment to money. Justice cannot be achieved, he wrote, without a more equitable distribution of money. The socioeconomic gap between whites and people of color is a part of systemic racism, but it also has roots in individuals' love of money and the security they believe it gives them. Although money is obviously a helpful tool that allows the human community to exchange necessary goods and services, we have allowed ourselves to become attached to it the way I am attached to my blanket: we believe we cannot be happy without it. Domínguez-Morano wrote that when people "lose money," they regard it not as the "loss of an outside object but a loss of something which has previously been 'incorporated'; that is, something intimately related with their egos."[13]

But this selfish clutching at material wealth does not reflect the love to which God calls us—and it is not the Ignatian way. Instead, Ignatius wrote:

> Love consists in a mutual sharing of goods, for example, the lover gives and shares with the beloved what he possesses, or something of that which he has or is able to give; and vice versa, the beloved shares with the lover. Hence, if one has knowledge, he shares it with the one who does not possess it; and so also if one has honors or riches. Thus, one always gives to the other.[14]

Father Pedro Arrupe, former head of the Society of Jesus, emphasized in a letter to the American Jesuits that love calls us to make societal changes requiring "courage of a high supernatural

[13] Domínguez-Morano, SJ, *Belief after Freud*, 212.

[14] Ignatius of Loyola, *The Spiritual Exercises of St. Ignatius: A New Translation* (New York: Vintage Books, 2000), 101.

order," as well as sacrifice, in order to realign "manpower and resources to meet the crying needs of our brothers in Christ who languish in racial degradation and inhuman poverty."[15] This is a level of radical sacrifice that asks us to go to the cross with Jesus and there let go of our egos' demands.

### Love: A Different Way of Being

When we act from a place of spiritual freedom, we can stop reacting from fear—and begin acting out of love. This interior personal work can be the beginning of societal change. We can begin to build Martin Luther King's "Beloved Community"—a place where every human being is affirmed and cared for. Racial healing is God's work in and through us. As Ignatius would say, it is a love that is shown in action.

During this third phase of *The Spiritual Exercises*, we see Christ willingly dying on the cross as a sign of justice and love. Christ endured the crucifixion not as an act of condemnation or judgment, but as an open door to a different way of interacting with one another, a different way of being—a way that is built on love.

### Decision Time

This third "week" is also what Ignatius calls a time of confirmation. As Jesuit author Gerald Fagan explains:

> You made a decision in the Second Week about how you are going to follow Jesus. Now Ignatius invites you to take that decision before Christ on the cross, to stand before the crucified Christ and say, "This is my decision." You stand at the foot of the cross and ask,

---

[15] Pedro Arrupe, SJ, *Selected Letters and Addresses: Justice with Faith Today* (St. Louis, MO: Institute of Jesuit Sources, 1979), 26.

"Can I be, am I going to be, a suffering servant the way Jesus is a suffering servant?"[16]

Are we willing to do all that we can so that all of us can breathe? Will we pray the litany of breath, having the courage to speak the names of those whom racism has killed? Will we allow ourselves to be changed by the suffering of Christ through the Black community?

When we can say yes to those questions, we are free to move on to the final phase of *The Spiritual Exercises*: the hope and possibility that is given expression in the resurrection of Jesus.

### Invitation to Discernment

Before you begin this Examen,[17] take a moment to imagine that you are with Jesus, a Black Jesus, and traveling with him to Jerusalem. Picture yourself sitting with him as he eats the last supper with his friends, and then follow him to the Garden of Gethsemane. Watch as he is betrayed and led to the cross. Finally, have the courage to imagine yourself at the foot of the cross, watching as Jesus gasps for breath. He is seeking to be treated not as threat but as a fellow human being, just as your Black sisters and brothers are seeking.

Now, in light of this experience, ask yourself:

- Have I fully loved God and fully loved my neighbor as myself?
- Have I caused pain to others by my actions or my words that offended my brother or my sister?

---

[16] Fagin, SJ, *Discovering Your Dream*, 51.

[17] This Examen is modified from "Examination of Conscience: A Look at Myself in the Mirror," a prayer resource for racial healing inspired by Pope Francis from the USCCB, Department of Justice, Peace & Human Development, https://www.usccb.org.

- Have I done enough to inform myself about the sin of racism, its roots, and its historical and contemporary manifestations? Have I opened my heart to see how unequal access to economic opportunity, jobs, housing, and education on the basis of skin color, race, or ethnicity has denied and continues to deny the equal dignity of others?
- Is there a root of racism within me that blurs my vision of Jesus in those who may seem different from me?
- Have I ever witnessed an occasion when someone was a victim of personal, institutional, systematic, or social racism and I did or said nothing?
- Have I ever been the one to inflict the pain of personal, institutional, systematic, or social racism?
- Am I willing to align myself with the presence of Christ in the Black community?

**Prayer**

*God, in your mercy,*
*show me my own complicity in injustice.*
*Convict me for my indifference.*
*Forgive me when I have remained silent.*
*Equip me with a zeal for righteousness.*
*Never let me grow accustomed or acclimated to unrighteousness.*[18]

[18] Rev. Dr. Yolanda Pierce, quoted in "Prayers for Racial Justice and Reconciliation," *JesuitResource.org*, https://www.xavier.edu.

# 12

# Resurrection

*I refuse to accept the view that mankind is so tragically bound to the starless midnight of racism and war that the bright daybreak of peace and brotherhood can never become a reality. . . . I believe that unarmed truth and unconditional love will have the final word.*

— Martin Luther King, Jr.,
Nobel Peace Prize Acceptance Speech, 1964

*The brown-skinned Jewish Jesus did not come to make us color blind, but that we might see each other for who we really are and see the deeper identity of bearing His image. This is our new identity. This is resurrection thinking. This is resurrection power.*

— Josh Buck,
"Race Relations and the Resurrection"

A few years ago, on Easter Sunday, I embarked on a quest for hope, seeking to find the grace to live as a Black man in the Society of Jesus within America. My destination was the

South, where I knew Blacks had a long history of suffering under the rope of racism. My Jesuit superiors did not fully understand why I felt the need to make this journey, and they were concerned about my safety. I, however, had spent a long period praying for discernment, and I was confident I was following God's will for my life. I knew I needed to come to terms with what God was asking of me from within the crucible of racism—and so I prayed for healing of the countless wounds left by the microaggressions I had experienced; I prayed that my eyes would be opened to a spiritual reality that would allow me to confront racism with interior awareness, trust, and an audacious belief in new possibilities.

When I reached New Orleans, my prayers were answered. There, in that magical city with all its charm, jazz, and French vibe, I felt at home. For the first time in years, I was with brothers and sisters who shared my skin color. Surrounded by a vibrant Black community, I regained a sense of my own identity.

While I was there, I met with the Auxiliary Bishop of New Orleans, Fernand J. Cheri, who shared his experience of being a Black man within the predominantly white Catholic Church. Before becoming a priest, he had been refused ordination multiple times due to the color of his skin. As he talked with me, I began to comprehend more fully the price a Black person pays because of racism. "Patrick," he said to me, "the Jesuits will just have to accept you with your blackness."

I had felt suffocated by the prejudice I had encountered since coming to America, but now Bishop Cheri's understanding and compassion breathed oxygen into my lungs. I realized he had not allowed racism to be a dead-end street going nowhere. Although Jesus suffers and dies anew in the crucible of racism, Bishop Cheri helped me understand that the Black community can also be a place of Resurrection.

The morning after this conversation, I woke up feeling as though I had been transformed. I was no longer someone ruled by skepticism and fear, caught in a vicious cycle of reaction to microaggressions. Bishop Cheri had given me back my roots, my connection to God through the Black community, and in doing so, I had become a new person—someone who was able to embrace possibility.

Racial injustice had left me traumatized. Afraid of being hurt still more deeply, I had allowed myself to become numb. Preoccupied with my selfish fears, I was blind to the reality of my Jesuit brothers. Now, however, I returned to the Society with a new perspective. I realized that the Jesuits in America are unavoidably infected by the disease of racism; they are a microcosm of the larger society that contains them. I understood that they too had been wounded by systemic racism. They were still growing, just as I was, and like me, they had both weaknesses and strengths.

As I focused on the possibility of healing, I found that my brothers began to accept me, despite their difficulties, as an act of love. Together, we could enter into a relationship built on trust, rather than fear and defensiveness. Together, we could say, "We are sinners who need grace. We are men who struggle with race relations. We need each other's prayers in order to move from '*jesuitica indifference*' to racial action."

My prayer life deepened as my imagination took fire. Committed to be an agent of change and reconciliation, I looked to the future with new hope. And all this evolved from the catalyst of a simple conversation, a conversation that led to a resurrection of divine love in my life.

## Joy

The fourth "week" of *The Spiritual Exercises* focuses on the joy of the Resurrection. That sense of exhilaration and possibility is the foundation of our call to share in Christ's mission of justice and reconciliation. During this phase of our spiritual journey, Ignatius directs us "to ask for the grace to rejoice and be glad intensely at so great glory and joy of Christ our Lord," as we "consider how the divinity, which seemed to hide itself in the passion, now appears and shows itself so marvelously in the most holy resurrection by its true and most holy effects."[1]

"To be glad intensely" is a keynote of Ignatian spirituality. The practice of following Christ that Ignatius taught is not a gloomy asceticism that focuses on guilt and sorrow; instead, it is the experience of "fullness of joy" in the Divine Presence (Ps 16:11), while all the while continuing to live in the physical world. During this fourth phase of the *Exercises*, we learn to find the Living God everywhere.

"*Resurrection*," wrote Jesuit author Kevin O'Brien, "refers to the event of God's transformation of life, making all things new, as in a new creation." He went on to note:

> We marvel at how Jesus in the resurrected life—where his divinity is no longer hidden—does very human things: eating, talking, consoling, teaching, and enjoying the company of others. As with the mystery of the Incarnation, we see in the Resurrection how our divinity and humanity are not opposed but are an integral part of each other.[2]

The divine perspective we encounter in this fourth phase of the *Exercises* is one of light and hope—but it is not a simplistic, pie-in-the-sky happiness that closes its eyes to real-world problems. And it is not easy. Like the other three stages of the *Exercises*, the fourth also challenges us to let go of our focus on our limited, selfish viewpoints; it requires a "persistent emptying of the self."[3]

---

[1] Ignatius of Loyola, *The Spiritual Exercises of Ignatius of Loyola*, trans. Elder Mullan, SJ (New York: P. J. Kenedy & Sons, 1914), 114.

[2] Kevin O'Brien, SJ, *The Ignatian Adventure: Experiencing the Spiritual Exercises of St. Ignatius in Daily Life* (Chicago: Loyola Press, 2011), 240.

[3] George Aschenbrenner, SJ, *Stretched for Greater Glory: What to Expect from the Spiritual Exercises* (Chicago: Loyola Press, 2004), 128.

**Dying to Our Selfishness**

The work of the fourth week is built on the dying to the self that is required in the third week. With Ignatius, we pray the "Suscipe" prayer:

> Take, O Lord, and receive all my liberty, my memory, my understanding, and my entire will. Whatever I have or hold, you have given me; I restore it all to you and surrender it wholly to be governed by your will. Give me only your love and your grace, and I am rich enough and ask for nothing more.

When we authentically enter into this prayer of Ignatius, we are not expressing an unhealthy self-flagellation or denying our identity as beloved children of God. Instead, through this prayer, we can begin to see Divinity more clearly. We let go of all that is less important in our lives in order to make room for that which is most important. We consent to the interior work of dying to selfishness, so that we can come to life in newer and fuller ways.

Jesuit theologian Karl Rahner connected the power of the "Suscipe" to the fourth phase of *The Spiritual Exercises*:

> Whoever can do that, whoever can say the "Suscipe" with his whole heart and soul and mean every word of it, whoever is capable of that because he is free from sin and has broken away from himself in the following of Christ, he has arrived at that point where St. Ignatius wants him to be at the end of the Spiritual Exercises. He is the kind of person St. Ignatius can send back into the world of daily life so that he can find the living God of love there in his work, in his destiny, in his gifts and sufferings, in life and death, in using and leaving the things of this earth. If he truly attains such love, he will

> possess God, not in opposition to the world, but as the only One who gives value and dignity to the world.[4]

### The Mortal Wound of Racism

The Bible speaks of the "Body of Christ" (1 Cor 12:27), and through this body, we experience Christ's death and resurrection. Racism has wounded that body; it has crucified it. The pain is so deep and so ancient that we struggle to find words for it. Meanwhile, many white people would rather pretend the pain no longer exists; they would like to claim that racism was a historical reality but not something that is real and present in the lives of twenty-first-century people of color. Such thinking is only possible when whites close their eyes to a vital part of Christ's Body, ignoring the Black community, which is impacted by racism on a daily basis. But we can't talk about Resurrection until we face the reality of racism. Until we repent of this evil, we are hiding a mortal wound. That is why we need the first three stages of the *Exercises* before we can reach the fourth—and even then, joy and hope don't come to us easily or automatically.

In this fourth stage, Ignatius asks us to enter into the stories of the risen Christ. As we do so, we notice how many times he comes to the people he meets with comfort and consolation. As we imagine Mary Magdalene at the tomb on the morning of the resurrection, the disciples walking along the road to Emmaus, and Jesus's followers huddled together in the upper room, we see people who are troubled and confused. They thought they were following Jesus to a destination of peace and triumph, but now they have watched their leader die, gasping for breath in agony. They are frightened and full of sorrow; they no longer know how they themselves can continue to breathe.

---

[4] Karl Rahner, SJ, *Spiritual Exercises*, trans. Kenneth Baker, SJ (South Bend, IN: St. Augustine's Press, 2014), 276–77.

People of color have also had this experience. Although Jesus taught only justice and love, whites have claimed the name of Christianity in defense of racism. In doing so, they put Jesus to death again, leaving us bewildered, angry, and confused. We cannot breathe in this atmosphere where the white Christ is used to justify hatred and violence.

### The Vision to See New Possibilities

In the Gospels, we read that after Jesus's resurrection, he comes to each of his friends and followers and speaks words of encouragement. He breathes on them and comforts their hearts. He helps them create a new creed of hope, a creed of possibility.

Here again, Ignatius teaches us that prayerful imagination is the necessary foundation for this new creed. Without it, we will be easily discouraged by everything we hear and read on the news, by the constant barrage of hatred and prejudice we experience in our own lives. Spiritual imagination empowers us to see a new reality—and then it energizes us to give flesh and bones to that reality. As Jesuit psychologist Domínguez-Morano wrote, "God cannot solve so many things without us, but prefers to stimulate us in search of a solution ourselves and to keep us company."[5] Spiritual imagination is how God keeps us company on the long road to justice.

Ignatius achieved great things in his life, but he, too, experienced discouragement and doubt. Shortly after his conversion, he heard the "voice of the enemy" taunting him, making him question whether he could find the strength to endure the rest of his life without the pleasures and addictions he had previously relied on for comfort. But Ignatius did not allow internal fears to control him. He confronted them directly; he realized they were mirages, without a foundation in the real would unless he gave it to them.

---

[5] Carlos Domínguez-Morano, SJ, *Belief after Freud: Religious Faith through the Crucible of Psychoanalysis* (New York: Routledge, 2018), 109.

Meanwhile, his spiritual imagination was a lens through which he could perceive divine reality.

As we follow Ignatius's example, we, too, can see the world as God intended it to be. We can experience joy and gratitude that racism will not have the final say in our world—and our gladness and thanksgiving empower us to do the work to make our vision flesh and blood.

I experienced the joy of the resurrection in 2008, when I learned that Barack Obama had been elected President of the United States. I turned on the television and saw people dancing in the streets, celebrating the achievement for the Black community that Obama's victory signaled. This was a moment of hope, of jubilation, as we caught a glimpse of what possibility thinking can create.

I saw on television that the mall in Washington was packed with people singing and dancing. I watched as people carried signs that said "HOPE" and "change we can believe in"—and I realized that I was seeing what the power of the imagination can achieve. A new story was unfolding—a story of liberation, unity, and justice.

That moment did not last. Obama's eight years of presidency did not magically end racism, and it was followed by four long years when racism was not only allowed but encouraged in ways it had not been for many years. And yet whenever I think of that day of hope and joy, I am encouraged again. God is always bringing justice into the world. God has done it in the past, and God will do it again, bringing new life out of ashes.

As I prayed for our world on that glad day in 2008, I imagined Mary Magdalene standing outside Jesus's tomb. Her face was shining with tears of hope and joy, and her hips were swaying, her feet dancing. Clutched in her hands was a sign that read "BLACK LIVES MATTER." I knew she carried that message not as a cry of protest but as an affirmation of a fundamental, human truth.

I felt renewed hope once again when I learned my own order, the Society of Jesus, has committed itself to the work of racial reparation. We have pledged to raise $100 million for descendants of the 272 enslaved women, men, and children sold by the Jesuit owners of Georgetown University in 1838. "Our shameful history of Jesuit slaveholding in the United States has been taken off the dusty shelf, and it can never be put back," said Tim Kesicki, SJ, who is president of the Jesuit Conference of Canada and the United States. He went on to say, "The lasting effects of slavery call each of us to do the work of truth and reconciliation."[6]

This call comes to us on the individual level, but we cannot accomplish it alone; we need the support and energy of others. In the days after the Resurrection, we see Jesus's followers come together and form a community that would go on to change the world. Today, justice still lives in community. The dynamism between the interior work and the work of the community is the dual focus of Ignatian spirituality. Through inner awareness and imagination, we contribute to the community—and through our interactions with others, we are inspired and empowered to continue our inner work. The transformation of the Resurrection changes us personally, even as we are energized to change the world.

In this Age of Breath, God is calling each of us to see that the struggle against systemic and personal racism is inseparable from our spiritual journey as followers of Christ. As Father Arrupe wrote:

> But in the zealous and persevering labors of this apostolate there will be the great consolation of hastening a new era in which all [humans] will have well-founded hope of living in the fullness of their God-given dignity. In meeting this challenge we will bear living and visible witness to the validity, the integrity, the

---

[6] Carol Zimmerman, "Jesuits Pledge $100 Million in Reparations to Descendants of Enslaved People," *National Catholic Reporter*, March 17, 2021.

> credibility and the relevance of the Christian message, in a world increasingly skeptical of the sincerity of Christians, if not of Christianity itself.[7]

### The Service of Love

At the end of the *Exercises*, Ignatius wrote that "we should value above everything else the great service which is given to God because of pure love." Ignatius did not believe that love was only an interior feeling but rather it embodied itself in the choices people make, in the way they actively love others. Through the work of justice, we give love back to the God who loves us. We enter into the divine work of bringing love to this earth.

"Now, in the Easter-risen life, the body of Jesus becomes a universal body that incorporates all of us within it," taught Jesuit theologian Pierre Teilhard de Chardin. "Despite our many disappointments and failures, joy and hope are always available when we recognize that we are living, moving, and enjoying life within the great Christ Body."[8]

From my place in Christ's Body, I have come to you with my story, the only context I have in which to reveal the crucible of racism as it exists in the world today. For me, this book has been a leap of hope. I pray that the Ignatian spirituality I love so much will encourage you to believe in the possibility of racial healing and inspire you to work for racial justice. May you be challenged to become aware, to enter into community, to feel compassion, to work for reconciliation—and to know the joy and possibility of the Resurrection.

My grandmother believed that tomorrow will always be better. It is just a matter of waiting to see what God will do. Hope has the last word.

---

[7] Pedro Arrupe, SJ, *Justice with Faith Today: Selected Letters and Addresses*, trans. Jerome Aixala (St. Louis, MO: Institute of Jesuit Sources, 1980), 27.

[8] Louis M. Savary, *The New Spiritual Exercises: In the Spirit of Pierre Teilhard de Chardin* (Mahwah, NJ: Paulist Press, 2012), 198.

**Invitation to Discernment**

Michelle Obama wrote:

> Race and racism is a reality that so many of us grow up learning to just deal with. But if we ever hope to move past it, it can't just be on people of color to deal with it. It's up to all of us—Black, white, everyone—no matter how well-meaning we think we might be, to do the honest, uncomfortable work of rooting it out. It starts with self-examination and listening to those whose lives are different from our own. It ends with justice, compassion, and empathy that manifests in our lives and on our streets. I pray we all have the strength for that journey.[9]

While reading this book, did you gain strength for the journey of justice? Ignatius invites us to practice "repetition" in prayer, by which we return to a previous prayer period in order to become more attentive to the movements of God in our heart. In that spirit, look back on what you have thought, felt, and prayed as you read this book.

- Become aware of how reading this book has made you feel.
- Review any ways that it has changed how you interact with others.
- Think about ways you could bring the ideas from this book into your daily life in the days to come.

---

[9] Michelle Obama, Instagram, May 29, 2020, https://www.instagram.com.

**Prayer for Dismantling Racism**

*Dear God, in our efforts to dismantle racism, we understand that we struggle not merely against flesh and blood but against powers and principalities—those institutions and systems that keep racism alive by perpetuating the lie that some members of the family are inferior and others superior.*

*Create in us a new mind and heart that will enable us to see brothers and sisters in the faces of those divided by racial categories.*

*Give us the grace and strength to rid ourselves of racial stereotypes that oppress some of us while providing entitlements to others.*

*Help us to create a Church and nation that embraces the hopes and fears of oppressed People of Color where we live, as well as those around the world.*

*Heal your family God, and make us one with you, in union with our brother Jesus, and empowered by your Holy Spirit.*[10]

---

[10] "Prayer for Dismantling Racism" written by the Pax Christi Anti-Racism Team. Used with permission of Pax Christi USA.

# Glossary

*Arrupe, Pedro*. Father Arrupe (1907–1991) was the twenty-eighth Superior General of the Jesuits (1965–1981). He was central to the Jesuit renewal after Vatican Council II and is considered the founder of the modern, post–Vatican II Society of Jesus. Father Arrupe spent twenty-seven years in Japan, where, at one point, he was suspected of being a spy and put in solitary confinement during World War II. He cared for victims of the atomic bomb in Hiroshima, and as Superior General, he started the Jesuit Refugee Service (JRS). He has been called the second founder of the Society, especially with regard to faith that works for justice.

*Consolation*. A "motion of the soul"—a state of mind or an emotional state—that tends to draw us closer to God. It also nourishes our relationships with others, encourages creativity and new ideas, restores our sense of equilibrium, allows us to see others more clearly, and releases new energy in us.

*De Mello, Anthony*. Born in Mumbai, India, Anthony De Mello started offering guided awareness exercises in the 1970s to Christians in both India and the United States. These exercises were eventually published as *Sadhana: A Way to God—Christian Exercises in Eastern Form* (Random House, 1978). Many more books followed until he died at age fifty-six. His book *Awareness* (Random House, 1992), which transcribes one of his workshops, is a good place to become acquainted with his approach. His basic message is a call to awareness—to wake up from the mental and spiritual sleep that most people live in without realizing it.

*Desolation.* A "motion of the soul"—a state of mind or an emotional state—that tends to separate us from God. It drains us of energy, severs relationships, makes us more focused on selfish concerns rather than the needs of others, and distorts our perceptions.

*Discernment.* Discernment of spirits interprets what Ignatius Loyola called the "motions of the soul," which include both consolation and desolation. These two interior movements consist of thoughts, imaginings, emotions, inclinations, desires, feelings, repulsions, and attractions. Spiritual discernment involves becoming aware of these movements, reflecting on them in order to understand where they come from and where they lead us, and then using this process as a foundation for decision-making.

*Disordered affections.* Ignatius used this term to describe our deep-seated desires for things that pull us away from God. When our desire for God is overpowered by our desire for other things, our affections are out of order; they are no longer structured according to a healthy and life-giving set of priorities. Ignatius taught that freedom from disordered affections is essential to following Jesus.

*Examen.* This is an opportunity for reflective prayer that helps us perceive the Divine Presence in all the people and events of each day. It usually includes these five steps: awareness of God's presence; a grateful review of the day; attention to our emotions; prayer; and looking toward the future. Ignatius taught his followers to practice this spiritual discipline twice a day.

*Formation.* Christian spiritual formation is the process of being shaped into the image of Christ for the glory of God and for the sake of others (see 2 Cor 3:17–18). For someone entering a religious order, the main purpose of formation is to discover our vocation and to shape our life in accordance with the spirituality of the community we seek to enter. The process of formation involves various steps, depending on the religious order. For a Jesuit, the formation steps include a Novitiate (two years), First Studies (three years), Regency (two to three years), Theology (three years), and Tertianship (several time options, such as two summers, one semester, or the better part of a year).

*General Congregation.* The supreme legislative body of the Society of Jesus, which consists of provincial superiors and locally elected representatives. It addresses major issues confronting Jesuit work and life, and it is also called to elect a new Superior General when the previous one dies or resigns.

*Gospel.* The "good news" about Jesus and his expression of God's unconditional love. The first four books of the Christian scriptures (Matthew, Mark, Luke, and John) are also referred to as "the Gospels," since they tell the story of Jesus.

*Grace.* Any unearned gift from God. Ignatius imagined it as an endless flow of divine love constantly issuing forth into all creation.

*Hopkins, Gerard Manley.* Considered to be one of the great lyric poets of the English language, Hopkins (1844–1889) used words to express his vision of God and the beauty of creation. He joined the Jesuits in 1868, and at first, he assumed his love of poetry should be abandoned so that he might serve God more wholeheartedly. His superior encouraged him to begin writing again, but his poems were not published until thirty years after his death. They then had a major impact on twentieth-century English poetry.

*Incarnation.* Giving flesh to spiritual reality, as Jesus did when he was born as a human baby.

*Indifference.* In *The Spiritual Exercises*, Ignatius encourages us to put aside personal preferences and attachments, becoming "indifferent" to them, so that nothing comes between us and God's desires for us.

*Kingdom of heaven.* This is the term Jesus uses in the Gospels for the reign of God, which he said was breaking into the world in the here and now, rather than in some distant afterlife. The kingdom of heaven is God's presence in the world creating healing, justice, love, and peace.

*Novitiate.* These are the very first years of religious formation. A Jesuit novice studies Jesuit history and Jesuit life; he makes the full *Spiritual Exercises* over thirty days; and he has other practical experiences, such as living among the poor, working in hospitals, going on pilgrimage, and/or working in a Jesuit-sponsored ministry while living in community with Jesuits who have completed their course of early formation.

*Province.* Provinces are geographic regions created for the purpose of governance within the Society of Jesus. The major administrator of each province is the Provincial, appointed by the Superior General for a period of six years.

*Rahner, Karl.* Rahner (1904–1984) was a German Jesuit, who is sometimes referred to as the father of Catholic theology of the twentieth century. In the 1960s, he was an important presence at Vatican II. His biographer, Geffrey B. Kelly, described Rahner's belief that God is "inspiriting the world to shape human destiny and to liberate people to see God in all things, in order to know in that freedom that their search for meaning can only end in God." For Rahner, the meaning of life cannot be separated from the ongoing experience of divine grace.

*Religious order.* A community of men or women bound together by the profession of vows such as chastity, poverty, and obedience, which are intended to be a way of following Jesus's example. This renunciation of things that are good in and of themselves is made for the sake of God's kingdom, as a witness against the societal abuse of sex, wealth, and power, and in order to be more available to a universal love that reaches beyond family ties, personal possessions, and self-determination.

*SJ* or *S.J.* These initials after a person's name indicate membership in the Society of Jesus.

*The Spiritual Exercises.* An organized set of spiritual practices put together by Ignatius of Loyola, based on his own personal experience. They invite us to reflect on central aspects of the Christian faith and especially to contemplate the life, death, and resurrection of Jesus. Ignatius intended *The Spiritual Exercises* to be a handbook that would help a spiritual coach guide a person engaged in the process outlined in the *Exercises.* As originally designed, *The Spiritual Exercises* would occupy a person full-time for four weeks, but even in the sixteenth century, Ignatius recognized that many people cannot step away from their responsibilities for that long a time, and so it is possible to do the *Exercises* part-time over a period of six to ten months. Ignatius worked on his little book for at least twenty-five years before it was finally published in 1548. Since then, millions of copies of *The Spiritual Exercises* have been sold around the world, and countless individuals have used the Exercises to grow spiritually.

*Spirituality.* The dictionary says that spirituality has to do with "churchy things," as well as reality that is invisible and intangible, altogether removed from the physical realm. Ignatius, however, would not agree. According to Ignatian thought, spirituality is the ability to perceive and interact with Divinity in all aspects of the world around us, both our internal and external realities. It is a way of living that orients us to the Spirit present in all things.

*Superiors*. These are people in authority within a religious order. Most religious orders are based on a hierarchy of authority, with the Superior General at the top.

"*Suscipe*." An ancient prayer that Ignatius included at the end of *The Spiritual Exercises*. The word *suscipe* is Latin for "receive." The words of the prayer are: "Receive, O Lord, all my liberty. Take my memory, understanding, and entire will. Whatever I have or possess you have given me; I restore it all to you, and surrender it wholly to be governed by your will. Give me love for you alone along with your grace, and I am rich enough, and ask for nothing more."

*Teilhard de Chardin, Pierre*. This French Jesuit is considered to be one of the great minds of the twentieth century. A paleontologist, Teilhard (1881–1955) synthesized the scientific theory of evolution with a Christian worldview. His respect and love for the Earth laid a foundation for modern ecologists.

*Theology*. The study of the nature of God and religious belief.

# Index